Delicious!

The Savvy Woman's Guide to
Living a Sweet, Sassy, and
Satisfied Life

Catrice M. Jackson

M.S., LMHP, LPC

FOR INFORMATION, CONTACT:
Catrice M. Jackson, M.S., LMHP, LPC
Speaker, Author, Delicious Life Designer and Master Chef

Please visit my websites at:
www.catriceologyenterprises.com
www.catricejacksonspeaks.com
www.catricemjackson.com

Online ordering is available for all products.

ISBN 978-0-615-33780-7
Library of Congress Control Number: 2010920370

Printed in the USA

10 9 8 7 6 5 4 3 2 1

Think about it... when was the last time you ate something *delicious?* What words describe how it tasted and looked, and what feelings or thoughts came to mind as you ate this delicious meal or food?

Did it make you feel satisfied, fulfilled, special, happy, joyful? When something is delicious, you want it, can't get enough of it, anticipate it, savor the flavor, and usually want more of it, right?

Things that are delicious are very appealing to the eye and tantalizing to the taste. Delicious things put a smile in your heart, make your soul sing and soothe your body with goodness...

Wouldn't you love to be a delicious woman? Yes, a DELICIOUS WOMAN! And live a delicious life?

Sure you would... and this is why:

A delicious life is
- Satisfying
- Fulfilling
- Sweet and savory
- Tasty and full of flavor
- One that makes your heart sing with joy and your soul smile with satisfaction
- One that you love, can't get enough of, anticipate and become consumed with. A delicious life is so good you want more and more.

Living behind a mask, or many masks, is way too much work. I say take them off, throw them away, reveal the real you! Share your juicy goodness with the world. I bet they will love the flavor of simply you!

Catriceology

There once was a woman who had a dream. She tried to work for people who didn't see the true value of her beautiful mind.

One day she walked to the edge of a cliff and decided she needed to learn how to fly or forever stay stuck in the captivity of someone else's box.

She knew she must be liberated from the things that kept her bound or never see the full beauty of what the world had to offer.

She knew she had to take the leap of faith, and without much thought she jumped off the cliff and instantly began to fly.

Immediately, despite her fears, she felt the freedom she had been longing for all her life. She was consumed with tremendous personal power and knew in that moment she could do anything she set her mind to.

Today she is living her life like it's vibrantly golden, staring fear in the face and saying "bring it on," and fully stepping into her personal power, awakened and alive in each moment. She loves her life, every sweet and savory moment of it, and is on a mission to help other women live a delicious life! I love my imperfect life, and you can, too!

The sweet life awaits you...

The Delicious Flavor
of Contents

Appetizers

The Main Menu (Chapters 1 through 16)

Dedication to a Delicious Woman

This book is dedicated to the most sassy woman I know: my grandmother, Dottie Hardgraves. In her eighties she is still as feisty as ever, and I love her for that. Although she is an older woman in the golden years of her life, she still lets you know "I am here, and I am one to be seen and heard!"

Thanks, Gran, for all the love you've shown over the years and for showing me how to be a strong and sassy woman! I took some special time to sit down with my grandmother to get some insight and wisdom about what it really means to be a woman. I knew before this moment that my grandma would tell it like it is, simply because she was and is a woman who always speaks her truth. Women of her time didn't sugarcoat anything; they spoke what was on their minds and if you didn't like it, it was going to be said anyway. I always loved that about my grandma when I was a kid, because half the time she said something that was so true and real it was funny. Grandma and I always had good times filled with so much laughter.

The interview began with me peeking through the windows of her soul, her eyes. I smiled at her, and she smiled back. I am deeply grateful to have her in my life and to have experienced the love only a grandmother can give. You know what I mean: when Momma told you no, Grandma figured out a way to make it a yes! My mother was and is a great mother, but times with Grandma were always uniquely special. I silently reflected upon our times together, then began to ask her the following questions.

My special moment with a deliciously sassy woman...

Q. Grandma, what does it mean to you to be a woman?
A. It means to be a good woman who is a praying woman who is active in her church, the community and the world. A good woman is a loving woman. A real woman loves her family no matter what.

I took some time to explain to her that I was writing a book about living a sweet, sassy, and satisfied life, and before I could finish, she laughed and said, "Ooh, that sounds like a good life, a life that God created." Indeed, she is correct, and one thing I know for sure about my Gran is that she loves God with all her heart. I then went on to tell her the title of the book was *Delicious,* and she said, "Delicious, that sounds good and I can tell you one thing for sure, God is delicious."

Q. What does the word *delicious* mean to you?
A. Delicious means that something is good, sweet, and tasty. It means something is so good you want more and can't wait to get more of it.

Q. Would you say that you are a sassy woman, and if so, why?
A. Yes! I am a sassy woman. I am quick to answer and tell it like it is. A sassy woman speaks her mind and sometimes people don't like it, but you must always speak the truth and not be afraid of what people will think of you.

Q. Have you lived a satisfied life, and if so, what made it satisfying?

A. Yes indeed, I have lived a satisfying and sanctified life all my life.

Q. When you think of the words "a delicious woman," what comes to mind?

A. A good life. A life that tastes good and has a lot of flavor. My life was delicious.

I am deeply grateful for the loving relationship I have with my grandmother. She is, and always will be, the most delicious woman I know. Thank you, Gran, for showing me what it means to be a delicious woman... a sweet, sassy, and satisfied woman. I love you.

Special Thanks

This delicious book would have not come to life without the love and support of my friends and family. Thank you for believing in my vision and my passion. I appreciate you!

Roy L. Jackson
Tahsahn Dennis
Robbie Jackson
Terri Sanders

Contributions

Book Cover Design: Charles Beason/Media Eyecon
Cover Photos: Brett Frerkes/ Echoes Inspired
    Photography
Editor: Janet Tilden/Executive Rewrites
Personal Executive Assistant: Terri Sanders

Delicious!

Appetizing

Delectable

Enjoyable

Heavenly

Luscious

Gratifying

Pleasant

Scrumptious

Savory

Titillating

Yummy

Now, that's the kind of life you deserve...

Who Is a Delicious Woman?

You know her; you've seen her. She is breathtaking; she is a phenomenal woman. When she walks into a room, the energy and attention immediately shift in her direction.

As she comes and goes, a sweet and delightful scent appears when she enters and follows her as she leaves. It is her *soul scent*. It is the mesmerizing aroma of her juicy goodness permeating the room. This delightful scent is the aroma of a woman who has courageously and intentionally done the work from the inside out, and she has become a delicious woman.

She is not perfect, nor does she strive to be. She is a woman who has completely embraced who she is, from the top of her head to the soles of her feet. She realizes that she is a work in progress, and she diligently works every day to become the woman she desires to be, a beautiful masterpiece of self.

A delicious woman is awesomely comfortable in her own skin. She has boldly stepped into her personal power. Living on auto-pilot is a thing of the past, and she refuses to allow anyone other than herself to control the quality, depth, direction, and flavor of her life.

A delicious woman is ready at all times to face and conquer her fears, knowing that fear will always be present yet she will stare it in the face. She does not allow the presence of fear to keep her immobilized in life.

A delicious woman has a clear and colorfully profound vision for her life. She knows what she wants and has designed a personalized recipe to achieve it. She is living the life of her dreams on her own terms. She does not make excuses for her life but takes full responsibility for the life she is living and the life she aspires to live.

A delicious woman lives in the *right now* moment with mindfulness, intention, and full sensory awareness. She speaks and breathes life into her dreams and the dreams of other women.

A delicious woman lives a delicious life because she is courageous enough to open up her life pantry, pull out her best ingredients, and use the "Seven Laws of Delicious Living" recipe (page xix) to create a sweet, savory, and satisfying life.

A delicious woman is a woman other people enjoy being around, and people often look forward to being with her. She has discovered her unique light and uses it to bring luminosity to those in her intimate circle and the world. She is a beacon of inspiration who inspires other women to become their best selves and to live their best lives.

The ingredients for becoming a delicious woman are different for each woman, and that's what gives each woman her uniquely designed flavor. Your deliciousness will be much different from that of other women, so it will be up to you to determine and create your own flavor.

Are you ready to become phenomenally delicious? Are you ready to discover and release your juicy goodness? Are you ready to finally live the life of your dreams? *It's time to get delicious.* No more excuses, no more blame, no more procrastination, and no more self-sabotage.

Delicious living is for ready women! I know you are ready, simply by the fact that you are reading this book. My philosophy is if you stay ready, you don't have to get ready. If life has given you lemons, don't whine about it; take those lemons and whip up the most delicious lemon meringue pie, serve it up on a sassy silver platter, and say with a smile, "You can give me all the lemons in the world, and I will still make something delicious out of them."

Preface

Are you living the life of your dreams? Does your life pulsate with energy? Do you feel alive inside, and are you doing what you love every day? If you answered "No" to these questions, it's time for you to become delicious from the inside out and create your delicious life. If you answered "Yes," then you are about to learn how to become even more delicious! There is no time like the present to begin crafting a life you love.

Quit complaining about your life—take responsibility and create a life that pulsates with radiant, colorful energy! It's really pretty simple: you can complain about your problems and misfortunes in life, or you can dry your eyes and get over yourself. This book is for not for the faint of heart or the sentimentalist; it is for those who are sick and tired of being sick and tired and those who are ready to get out of the passenger seat and drive the damn car. This book is for women who are *ready* to live life out loud, fully awake and present in each moment. This book is for you. Are you ready to create a deliciously fabulous life?

Life is not as complicated as we make it. All we are required to do is wake up, love ourselves, give back to the world, show gratitude, and live our divine purpose. If you simply do these five things, what else is left? If you wake up, that is half the battle. If you wake up loving yourself, faults and all, you have accomplished something amazing. If you give back to the world unselfishly, everything you desire will come back to you tenfold. If you show gratitude, the universe will bless you more abundantly, and if you live on purpose, your provisions will be met. Doesn't this sound like a wonderful life? Well, it is, and there's no special secret to having a life like this, other than saying today, right now: "I will stop making life so complicated and create the life I desire through simple actions."

Who promised you that life would be easy? Who told you that you would not have to weather a storm or two in your life? Who told you that relationships are guaranteed to be perfect? Who told you that people are absolutely going to treat you the same way you treat them? I am amazed at how many people believe that these fallacies are written in a book somewhere and all human beings are required to read this so-called book and adhere to the rules. This is idealistic thinking, and while I too am an idealist, my experiences tell me that human beings are far too complex to believe in a set of rules that people will follow. Yes, I know there are some who would and do follow such rules. If you are ready to end the pain, suffering, misery, unhappiness, or complacency in your life, then it's time to get into reality with a capital R.

This book is your recipe book for a delicious life. The short stories, life reflections, and simple acts of revealing your *delicious vibrancy* in life will compassionately challenge you to always be in the driver's seat of your life. Fasten your seatbelt and get ready for a candid, insightful, and simple ride to revealing the radiant, vibrant, and delicious woman within.

If you truly desire to be a sassy, savvy, and satisfied woman, then read this book and use it to create a tasty life you love. You don't have to wait for the "blissful life to come;" you are the creator of your reality, and you are the one who is responsible for your life. Walk by faith and take steps in the dark. That means move; don't stand still. You must take one step at a time and move forward every day. Joy is waiting for you to peel away the layers of gloom and doom so it can be deliciously luminous in your life.

The time is NOW for joyful living! Enough is enough—this is *your* time to create a life you love, a vibrant life full of excitement, energy, and radiance. I want you to commit to vibrant living from this point on and know you can do what you want to do, be who you want to be, and live how you want to live… if you choose!

You have two choices: live your life as it is, or take control of your destiny. Everything you need to create a life you love is within you. All you have to do is go deep within your life cupboard and pull out the inner ingredients you already have and whip up a sweet and savory life. Does that sound too simple? Well, it is simple, so don't make it complicated. Just believe you deserve it, and do it!

In my first book, *Soul Eruption! An Amazing Journey of Self-Discovery,* I provided a blueprint for living, a guide for people to tap into their inner jewels and begin living life with no limits. If you have not read *Soul Eruption,* I suggest you do so, as it will be a wonderful prerequisite to creating and living a vibrantly delicious life. The purpose of that book was to help people experience a soul eruption, an awakening of the inner eye—a clear and profound moment when everything becomes crystal clear and you discover who you are, why you exist, and your purpose for living.

Here are the five essential signs that you have not experienced a soul eruption:

1. You feel numb inside and may describe your life as empty, confused, dark, lonely, or foggy.
2. You are living on auto pilot: going to a job you hate, doing the same old routine every day, and lacking energy and excitement in your life.

3. You have no idea what your purpose is in life. You are unsure why you exist and what your mission in life might be.
4. You are envious of the lives that other people have.
5. You are living in fear, afraid to take the leap of faith, scared to take risks and take control of your life.

Does this sound like you or your life? If you are experiencing any one of the five signs, it's time to create a delicious life you love, and this book will help you do that. You may be thinking, "What does a deliciously vibrant life look like?" I have a few answers, and you'll discover the rest as you read this delectable book...

- You wake up energized and ready to face the world.
- You stare fear in the face and say "Bring it on."
- You push through your fears and take baby steps towards the creation of your destiny.
- You see the positive in people.
- You feel confident inside, regardless of the situation.
- You are living on purpose and know exactly why you exist.
- You have pep in your step and see the possibilities and opportunities in each day.

Before you begin the journey of creating your vibrant life, there are some important questions you must ask yourself. Your answers to these questions will be instrumental in your ability to create a life you love—a life on your own terms. Do not cheat yourself by writing down responses that are not true. You must dig deep.

25 questions to help you begin creating your delicious life...

(See pages 157 to 164 for space to answer these questions.)

1. Am I living the life of my dreams?
2. Is my life in balance?
3. Is someone or something controlling my life, other than me?
4. What are my biggest fears?
5. Am I willing to take a deep look into my soul and discover why I exist?
6. How am I showing gratitude in my life?
7. Am I giving back to the world?
8. If I could do anything and not have to worry about money, what would I be doing?
9. Who is creating stress in my life?
10. Do I wake up excited about the day or dread getting out of bed?
11. What makes me feel alive inside?
12. Am I living in faith or living in fear?
13. If I lose my job, do I have a backup plan?
14. Have I created my "sweet life list" (a list of the things I want to do, experience, and accomplish in life before I die)? (See pages 155–156.)
15. Am I living in the moment or stuck in the past?
16. Is my life pulsating with energy?
17. If I don't wake up tomorrow morning, have I done everything I wanted to?
18. What is the vision for my life?
19. Have I identified the people who are in my life for a reason, a season, and a lifetime?
20. Am I ready to take back my life?

21. Do I speak my truth every day?
22. Is my spirit authentic?
23. Am I listening to my authentic voice?
24. Who am I allowing to steal my emotional energy?
25. Am I working at a job or loving my career?

Exploring these critical questions and finding the answers to them will be the foundation for creating a sweet life you love. Throughout this book you will be challenged to seek the answers to these questions through reflections on life, stories, and exercises designed to help you determine what really matters in your life and provide you with a compass creating a vibrant life. You'll notice that I use the words *vibrant, radiant,* and *delicious* (or forms of them) interchangeably. In my opinion it's all the same. Vibrant (or radiant) people are attractive, magnetic, saucy, and sassy, and people often "thirst or hunger" for more of their appealing personality, therefore making them delicious. So whether you want to become vibrant, radiant, or delicious, this book will help you tap into your "sweet and savory" core and share it with the world.

A delicious woman is vibrant, liberated, hopeful, intentional, willing, courageous, satisfied, loving, joyful, bold, balanced, self-preserving, in control, present, magnetizing, charismatic, and phenomenally unique. The recipe for a delicious life contains these ingredients.

*"It's time for you to become **delicious** from the inside out."*

Catriceology's Seven Laws of Delicious Living Success

Delicious Law #1: Stop letting other people, events, and your life situation control who you are or who you want to become.

Delicious Law #2: Quit living in fear, doubt, and worry!

Delicious Law #3: Dream BIG and have even bigger faith.

Delicious Law #4: Take control of your thoughts. Think your way to the life you desire.

Delicious Law #5: Discover your "it," master it, and shamelessly flaunt it to the world.

Delicious Law #6: Reinvent yourself each day.

Delicious Law #7: Stop making excuses, and just live your life and make sure it's delicious...

If you begin using these Seven Delicious Laws as your guideposts for living, I am confident that you will discover and release your juicy goodness. You will discover your unique, personal ingredients and create the recipe to live your most fabulously delicious dream life. These laws are designed to be simple, practical, and effective because living the delicious life and becoming a delicious woman is not rocket science. In fact, it's fairly easy if you believe you deserve it and dedicate your time, energy, and resources to becoming your most delicious self from the inside out. I will explain these laws in more depth and sprinkle "delicious law" tidbits throughout the book.

Chapter 1
Discover and Define Your Unique Flavor

Vibrancy is when you leave a lasting impression on someone without saying a word...

Vibrant means lively, vivacious, pulsating, alive, bright, energetic!

Living a vibrantly delicious life does not require a master plan or mysterious methods. Vibrancy is often described as a colorful vibration of pulsating energy. Vibrancy means that you are living in the moment, living without fear, and living with a full awakening. Vibrancy allows you to wake up every day and be excited about life. Vibrancy means that you are lively, energetic, excited, and filled with joy, passion, zest, and happiness.

Here is what vibrancy looks like in real life:

1. You wake up energized, ready to face the world.

2. You stare fear in the face and say "Bring it on."

3. You push through your fears and take baby steps toward the creation of your destiny.

4. You see the positive in people.

5. You feel confident inside, regardless of the situation.

6. You are living on purpose and know why you exist.

7. You have pep in your step and see the possibilities and opportunities in each day.

8. You go to bed satisfied, knowing you have done your best in any given day.

9. You light up the room, and people know you exist.

10. You speak from your compassionate and honest voice.

11. You attract people into your life because your personality is magnetic.

12. You feel alive inside because you are doing work you love.

13. You create your life on your own terms.

14. You do not let worldly negativity affect your personal outlook on life.

15. You do everything very passionately.

16. You have a clear, vivid, and colorful vision for your future.

17. You feel good about your outer appearance and work to keep your personal image polished.

18. You live to give and find ways daily to inspire others towards their highest self.

19. You are spiritually awakened and listen and respond to your intuitive voice.

20. You love life and are open to the wonderful discoveries and opportunities that await you.

Delicious!

Of the twenty characteristics listed on pages 1–2, how many do you have? _____

List each missing characteristic by number, and then write down why this description does not apply to you.

Number   *Reason*

_____   _____

             _____

_____   _____

             _____

_____   _____

             _____

_____   _____

             _____

_____   _____

             _____

When was the last time you heard someone describe you using any of the following words?

Glowing, Radiant, Energized, Vibrant, Delicious, Stunning, Brilliant, Luminous, Exciting, Inspirational, Powerful, Joyful, Peaceful, Graceful…

Better yet, when was the last time *you* used words like that to describe yourself? If you are not regularly hearing or using these words or similar words, why not?

Chapter 1: Discover and Define Your Unique Flavor

Without a doubt, these descriptions fit you in your own way. They may be very evident, or they may be buried under self-defeating thoughts. This chapter is designed to help you discover and determine what *deliciously vibrant* means to you. You are unique, and therefore your definition of delicious living has to be yours, on your own terms. I want you to purely focus on you: what you need, what you desire, and how you want to BE in life. It's time to be liberated from the things that bind you. It's time to release your beautiful, wise, vibrant, radiant, and delicious self.

When you think about living a vibrant life, what comes to mind? One word in particular comes to mind for me, and that is the word *radiance*. Radiance is not only about an outer glow, but more importantly about your inner glow. Radiance is about your inner beauty, the glow or energy you emanate or project into the world. Radiance shows up in your personality, intelligence, grace, congeniality, charm, integrity, congruency, and personal elegance. Radiance, in other words, is the result of how you feel about yourself on the inside and how those feelings affect your outward appearance and behavior. Your radiance is the "juicy goodness" hidden behind the layers and masks you may be wearing.

When you look in the mirror, do you see a radiant woman? Stop right now and go stand in front of the mirror and take a look at yourself from various angles. Then come back and take an inventory. Write down whether you saw each of the following characteristics. (Don't cheat by looking at the list before you go to the mirror.)

What did you see in the mirror?
(Check all that apply.)

_____ Bright eyes

_____ Joyful expression

_____ Luminous skin

_____ Brilliant and glowing hair

_____ A beaming soul shining through

_____ A sense of love of the skin you're in

_____ A beautiful woman staring back at you

_____ An image that emanates positive, glowing energy

If you did not see some of these characteristics, don't worry. They are there. You just have to dig deep, discover them, and release them into the world. Radiance shows up in your voice, appearance, facial expressions, attire, body language, and silent presence. Discovering and releasing your juicy, radiant self is easy to do if you are willing to do the work from the inside out to reveal it. The next set of questions will help you go a little deeper to discover whether you see and believe that you are a radiant woman.

Take a moment to answer the following questions.

1. When I walk into a room, do people notice me?

2. When I am part of a group, do I stand out?

3. Have I ever been told I was a radiant woman? If so, when?

4. Do people seem to be naturally or automatically attracted to me?

5. When I speak, do people stop and listen?

6. Have I ever been told that I am a magnetic person or that people are drawn to me?

Now here comes the important part. It's time to determine what *radiant* and *delicious* mean to you so you can have a clear picture of what you desire to become and create a life plan to achieve this state of being. Take a few moments to think about a radiant or delicious woman you know, or to recall the last time you were in a group of people and there was one woman who just seemed to stand out or attract others. Maybe you can reflect upon a woman you've admired from afar and use that as guide to help you determine what kind of radiant and delicious woman you want to become. If you are having difficulty coming up with characteristics of a radiant woman or defining *delicious* or *radiant* for yourself, consider the questions below.

- What does a radiant woman look like? (physical presence)

- How does a radiant woman live her life? (actions and behavior)

- How does a radiant woman think? (spiritual and emotional energy)

Delicious!

- What famous or not-so-famous women come to mind when you think of a radiant woman? (List them here and write one thing you admire about each one.)

You may be wondering why I am asking you to reflect on other women when this book is supposed to be about you. In my work as a coach, counselor, and speaker, I have found that it is particularly difficult for some women to see their own beauty, power, and character. These questions are not intended to help you become a carbon copy of someone else, but rather to help you tap into what "matters" to you, what you admire and appreciate about being a woman, what you appreciate about yourself that may be hidden, and or who you want to become in your journey of self-transformation. So embrace the challenge, and think deeply and critically about your life—what you want, who you want to become, and how you want to live your life.

The goal of this book is to help you become a delicious woman from the inside out, and therefore you will have to do some work. I realize this may be difficult or challenging, but if you really want to live your most delicious life you will dedicate your time, energy, and resources to doing just that. Becoming delicious from the inside out requires you to be courageous enough to look deeply into your soul and acknowledge your strengths and limitations.

Critical Questions (Take some time to answer each question.)
1. How do I show up in the world? Am I confident, assertive, aware, and engaged?

2. What silent messages am I sending to other people? Am I competent, smart, joyful, and excited?

3. When I am with other people, what messages do they send me about my presence? Are they interested, bored, excited, captivated, and engaged?

4. How often during my day am I sought out, complimented, approached, and noticed?

A delicious woman silently and sometimes openly emanates a radiant vibration of warm, colorful, intriguing, lively, exciting, and passionate energy. A vibrant woman

Delicious!

thinks with optimism, clarity, focus, and intention. A vibrant woman is purposeful and aware of who she is and how she shows up in the world. A delicious woman acts with integrity and from her core values. She is strategic, graceful, and truly believes that all is well and she deserves what life has to offer. A vibrant woman pulsates with energy. She is joyful, hopeful, and alive, and it shows in her daily behavior. She is a passionate, purpose-driven woman who navigates in the world with ease and grace. A delicious woman knows the significance of her personal power and steps into it every day with full attention to creating and living a life she loves.

One of the greatest things about a delicious woman is her awareness of the value and urgency of preserving her emotional energy. Therefore, she is extremely careful, selective, and mindful about whom she allows into her inner circle. She knows who feeds her emotional energy and who depletes it. A delicious woman knows how critical it is to restore and rejuvenate her emotional energy and therefore practices daily self-care rituals to sustain it. Finally, a delicious woman is a go-getter, an obstacle buster, a woman on the move who takes daily actions in creating her reality through the power of intention, reflection, and action.

Like beautiful skin, some women are born with inner radiance while others must work to reveal it. Nevertheless, one thing is certain: there is a radiant being in all of us. If you are blessed to be a naturally radiant woman, congratulations. If not, your radiance is waiting to be revealed. It may take some work, but you are worth the effort.

That beautiful, radiant woman you seek to become can be revealed in three transformational steps. These techniques apply to your inner beauty as well as your outer skin.

Here are three techniques that can help you to reveal both your outer and inner radiance:

1. **Exfoliate:** slough away the dead skin. (Let go of things that have no value or weigh heavily upon you.)

2. **Hydrate:** add moisture. (Protect and rejuvenate your self-image.)

3. **Nourish:** be sure to get enough vitamins. (Restore and replenish your energy level.)

To **exfoliate** means to detach or shed. Exfoliation helps remove dead cells and speeds up the process of revealing more translucent, glowing, healthy skin. When you exfoliate, you detoxify your skin and rid it from impurities, dirt, and the harmful effects of wind and sun. To exfoliate your spirit, you must first identify the things that have no meaning in your life, the things that weigh heavily upon you. These elements could include people, places, things, events, or expectations. To do identify them, answer the following questions.

- What is dead weight in my life?

- What or who is weighing heavily upon me?

- Who or what is blocking or dulling my shine?

Answering the questions above is essential to your exfoliation success. I know it can seem overwhelming to

Delicious!

think about the answers; however, either you reveal what's stealing your shine or remain a dull woman living a dull life. It's your choice. I know you desire to be radiant, so face your fears and tackle those questions with clarity and honesty. Once you've exfoliated (removed the dead stuff) it's time to re-hydrate your open, clean, and maybe even vulnerable skin (spirit).

Hydrating (moisturizing, rejuvenating) your skin is an essential step in revealing your inner and outer glow. Hydration protects your skin (spirit) and helps it become and remain supple and full of elasticity. Think of it this way. Your outer skin can be considered a canvas on which you display all the beautiful things about you, such as your hairstyle, jewelry, makeup, smile, clothes, and so on. How you adorn this outer canvas is an indication of how you feel about and adorn your inner canvas. Keeping your outer canvas hydrated increases its elasticity—the ability to be flexible and resilient. It's just as important to moisturize and rejuvenate your inner canvas (spirit) so that when you have valley moments or challenging moments in life, your spirit will not crack under the pressure.

Physically speaking, water and moisturizing creams are the best two sources of hydration for your skin. Water feeds your cells, improves circulation, and increases organ function and movement. The same is true with regard to hydrating your spirit. You must put into yourself things that feed you, keep you moving, and enhance who you are in your core.

Nourish: According to dermatologists, vitamins C and E are essential for healthy skin. Vitamin C is a powerful antioxidant that fights off free radicals or disease-causing cells. From a spiritual perspective, vitamin C is your sunshine and your life and energy source.

Okay, now it's time for some more challenging questions. Take a few minutes to answer the questions that follow. Be completely honest with yourself, even if the people who come to mind are those in your intimate circle, including family members and friends.

- Who or what is keeping me stuck, immobilized, or dysfunctional?

- Who or what feeds my soul, mind, and spirit?

- Who or what replenishes me when my spirit is dry and thirsty?

- What or who protects me from the dangerous or toxic elements of the world?

- Who or what restores my glow?

- What or who brings happiness and light to my life?

- What or who gives me energy and makes me feel alive?

- What tools do I have to fight off toxic people?

Delicious!

At this point, I hope you have been successful at a few things:

1. You've defined what *delicious* and *radiant* looks like for you.
2. You've discovered who or what is dulling your life.
3. You've realized the importance of protecting your inner skin as well as your outer skin.
4. You've begun to create a plan to exfoliate the dead "stuff" out of your life.
5. You've begun to realize the importance of ridding yourself and your life from the people who keep you stuck and in dark places.

This transformation won't happen overnight. You'll have to exfoliate every day and maybe even several times a day if you truly desire to slough away the people, places, and events that are preventing your radiant, vibrant, and delicious self from shining through. The exercises and tips in the following chapters will continue to provide you with techniques to slowly reveal your inner and outer juiciness. The first step in becoming a deliciously vibrant woman is believing that you deserve and are able to live a sweet and savory life!

Delicious Living Tip #1

A savvy woman sits in the driver's seat of her life. The life you are living is a reflection of your dominant thoughts. You can transform your life anytime you choose. Get back in the driver's seat of life and soar into your destiny!

Chapter 1: Discover and Define Your Unique Flavor

Food for Thought

What ingredients did you extract from this chapter to create your own recipe for a delicious life? Use the space below to record your thoughts.

Delicious!

Chapter 2
Take Back Your Life

Liberation means knowing your truth, speaking your truth, and refusing to remain captive within yourself…

It means being *free, released,* and *unshackled!*

Becoming well from the inside out is one of the most powerful and effective ways to release your inner radiance. Releasing your inner radiance is pivotal in becoming a deliciously vibrant woman and creating a life you love.

A joyful life comes from within. Joy is not something you should outwardly seek; joy lives within you, and you can be joyful any time you choose. The difference between happiness and joy is that happiness is circumstantial whereas joy is a state of being. You can be happy in various settings or moments in time, and when that time has expired and you are no longer in that setting happiness will fade.

When you are fully and truly joyful you feel joy all the time, no matter the circumstances. Yes, joy fades; yet it still lies within you. You have to work to keep your joy alive, thriving and pulsating with energy.

It's time now to do the work… the sometimes difficult task of working from the inside out. It's time for you to believe you are worthy, beautiful, and that all is well and you deserve to live a delicious life. As you move through this book, pay attention to the primary limiting beliefs you have about yourself—the beliefs that keep you from knowing for sure that all is well and you deserve to live a life you love. You must become very mindful of these beliefs, as they hold the power in whether you stay stuck in life or become liberated from self.

I challenge you to change every negative or limiting belief into a positive affirmation or intention statement for your life. It's time for you to take back your life from the things that are holding you back.

I strongly believe that what you think of yourself matters most, yet it is often important to get feedback from those who love us in order to determine how we are showing up in the world. Now, don't get too caught up in what other people think about you, but rather park their comments in the back of your mind to use as a gauge of your personal presence in the world. At the conclusion of this chapter I will ask you to identify three people who know you well, people that you love and trust, and ask them to describe you or how you show up in the world and see if any words related to radiance come up.

Here are a few suggestions for taking back your life:

1. Determine what or who is controlling your life and destiny.
2. Create a vivid mental picture of how you would like your life to be. Be very specific in envisioning where you live, who you are with, how you spend your time, what is your financial condition, and so on. Your mental picture must be very clear and detailed to help you attain what you are seeking.

Delicious!

3. Find a mentor. Look for someone who is living the life of her dreams and or in control of her life.
4. Get a coach! A coach can help you find clarity, set goals, create balance, and make your dreams a reality.
5. Become very intentional about your life. Only give energy to things and people that really matter to you.

When you think, live and act with intention you utilize all of your senses to fully experience each moment. When we operate on auto-pilot we miss the complexities and beauty of living. It is difficult to create the life you want if you function each day on cruise control. You must be present and fully awake in every moment.

It is time to wake up and take control of your life and stop letting other people and events construct your destiny. You may be wondering how to do that. It's clear and simple. The only thing that is complex about it is whether you will follow these simple suggestions or not.

17

Four simple yet complex actions to take back your life:
- Stop letting people determine your mood for the day or steal your joy.
- Stop letting your spouse, boss, or children drive you crazy.
- Stop worrying about what people might say about you.
- Stop settling for life as it is, instead of creating the life you want.

There is a battle going on inside each of us every day. Everyone on some level is struggling to claim victory over the internal voices that tell us we are not worthy, we are not good enough, we must settle for less. These messages go on and on. Sometimes this war can be overwhelming, and for some the internal voice wins. It wins because we allow it to. Even the best of us fall victim to the power of internal messages, but there is a stronger voice that we must learn to tap into: our own personal power.

Here's the difference: the voice of self-doubt lives in your mind, whereas the voice of personal power lives in your soul, your spirit. It is critical that you identify these adversarial voices and align your primary thoughts, feelings, and actions with the voice of personal power. Self-doubt will sabotage your relationships, keep you from reaching your goals, and force you to procrastinate on creating the life you desire. The voice of personal power tells you that you can, you will, and you are. Now is the time for you to claim victory over self-doubt.

Here are a few simple strategies to win the battle of self-doubt:

1. Identify the daily negative messages that play inside your head. Pick the primary messages, and write each one down on a separate sheet of paper.

2. For each message, determine the source from which it came (in other words, why do I think this way, who has told me this before, and what happened that has caused me to think this way?).

3. For each message, determine whether it is based on your deep beliefs about yourself or whether someone else has caused you to believe it. If it is not your original thought, disregard it because it doesn't matter what other people think.

4. Spend most of your attention on the messages that you believe to be true. Rewrite each one to turn it into a positive message. For example, if you have a deep belief that you are not worthy, change that thought to "I am worthy."

Delicious!

5. Each time a negative message enters your thoughts, reverse it and turn it into a positive thought. Repeat it daily as many times as it takes for you to truly believe it.

6. Since personal power comes from your soul, you must work every day to nourish and strengthen your spirit. It is essential that you keep this place sacred and alive. Discover what makes your soul feel good, and do more of (for example, reading, music, nature, giving back to others, and so on).

Claiming victory over self-doubt can be a challenge, but you can win the battle if you choose. Spend your days thinking about the positive things in your life, remembering past accomplishments, and specifically envisioning how you want your life to be. As you focus on what you want versus what you have, you will begin to turn those wants or dreams into reality.

You must go beyond thinking and move quickly into intentional action. That means you must do something every day to create the life you want. It doesn't have to be anything drastic for you to begin creating a delicious life. For example, you can simply start being more aware in your daily interactions. Listen closely to what other people are saying, notice their facial expressions, make eye contact with them, and pay attention to their body language.

You should also start paying closer attention to how you feel when you are around certain people and in certain situations. Learning to listen to your body and how it responds to people, places, and situations is the best way to align with your soul. When you get those gut feelings that say "This isn't right" or "That person makes me feel uncomfortable or irritated," you must listen to that voice, because it is your soul or intuition speaking. Your soul is your compass for living and creating the life of your dreams. Awaken it, connect with it, and listen to it because everything you need to be happy and successful you already have within you.

Creating a deliciously vibrant life is all about the power to choose. You can continue to live your life like it is or create one that pulsates with energy, a life you love, the life of your dreams. You must become very intentional in your choices. You must start paying close attention to your intuitive voice, the voice that is wise, compassionate, and loving. You'll know when your intuitive voice is speaking because it just feels right. The messages from this voice are flexible, freeing, comforting, and all-knowing.

As you begin making decisions about your life, use your intuitive voice as your guide for navigating in the world. Listening to your intuitive voice is a skill, an art that you can develop. So I pose a challenge for you as a beginning exercise in developing the art of intuitive living. I want you to fully engage in the exercise below and then record your thoughts and behaviors as you move through the exercise.

Take the 24-Hour Intuitive Living Challenge

For one full day, make decisions based on what feels right. Make decisions only if they are going to intentionally change your life for the better. In other words, if the outcome of your decision is going to change the direction of your life and or take you to the next level, then do it; if not, maybe you should do something different. (For example, arguing with your partner about the same old stuff is only going to keep you stuck and immobilized, so

Delicious!

don't argue. Instead, direct your emotional energy toward your goals in life.) It's important that you only give energy to things that matter, and that means demonstrating the ability to say no, mean no, and not feel guilty about it. Listen to your inner voice everywhere you are and with every person with whom you share space. Listen... the answers are there. Follow the lead of your intuitive voice and respond with confidence, ease, and grace. Do not second-guess your intuitive voice; remember that it is wise, compassionate, and all-knowing.

After taking the 24-hour intuitive challenge, write about your experiences here.

There is no time like the present moment to begin transforming your life. You must take action right now, despite your worries, doubts, and fears. The sweet life you desire is right in front of you; it's within you and you can walk out your destiny anytime you choose. Taking action means facing your fears and taking baby steps towards creating a life you love. You must get very clear, focused and intentional about your life and begin doing things within your power *right now*, not tomorrow.

Take a few moments and think about the desires of your heart. Think about how you want to BE in life, not about what you want to do. Think about the people, tasks, or things that are standing in the way of living life on your own terms. Think about ten actions you can take right now to achieve that state of being.

1. Identify how you want to BE and FEEL.
2. Identify one intentional act you can do to get that feeling or state of being.
3. Identify the expected outcome; in other words, describe the benefit of this new state of feeling and being.
4. Commit to doing these actions for 30 days. Record the changes in how you think, feel, act, engage with others, and live your life. (Use the chart on pages 23–24.)

(To get you started, here's an example of how to use this chart)

What feeling do I want to feel?	What can I do right now to get that feeling?	What is the overall outcome expected?
Physical vitality, lightness, and wellness	*Put away the scale and focus on feeling and looking better versus how much the scale says.*	*Less worry and stress about a number that does not define me. I will learn to listen to my body.*
Peaceful and knowing	*Let go of all the things I do not have direct control over and purely focus on how I am "being" in the world.*	*I will give energy to all the things that really matter and liberate myself from worry, stress, and doubt.*

Delicious!

What feeling do I want to feel?	What can I do right now to get that feeling?	What is the overall outcome expected?

Chapter 2: Take Back Your Life

What feeling do I want to feel?	What can I do right now to get that feeling?	What is the overall outcome expected?

Delicious!

Delicious Living Tip #2

A savvy woman takes good care of herself. Take time to get quiet, be still and REALLY think about your life. Simply STOP, get off the treadmill of life, and listen to your inner voice. What is it saying?

Chapter 2: Take Back Your Life

Food for Thought

What ingredients did you extract from this chapter to create your own recipe for a delicious life? Use the space below to record your thoughts.

Delicious!

Chapter 3
Put Your Sassy Stilettos on and Walk It Out

Hope is believing in yourself
when everything and everyone
around says you can't...

Hope: desire, aspiration, trust, faith, optimism, anticipation!

27

As you work through this book to create your delicious life, you will be on a journey... a soul journey. A *soul journey* is an intimate, honest, and intentional ongoing dialogue with self that each of us must experience in our lives. Taking a soul journey is essential for discovering who you are in your core and crafting a life of passion and purpose. Taking a soul journey is not always an easy thing to do. A soul journey challenges you to look at things in your past and present life that may be causing you pain and unhappiness. Going on a soul journey can be frightening and create emotional uncertainty, yet you must embark upon this journey into your soul despite the pain and challenges so that you can heal your wounds, become enlightened, and live the life you desire.

While you're on this journey called life, on occasion you'll find yourself in the valleys: places where you feel unsure, stagnant, confused, alone, or lost. While you are in one of these valleys, all you can think about is how to get to the mountaintop. Instead, you must expend your energy on taking one step at a time toward the base of the mountain.

In your times of rest, it is essential that you reflect upon why you are in the valley. How did you get there, have you been here before, and what did you do to get out the last time?

People end up in valleys for various reasons. Either they are not paying attention along their journey and end up on a path that they didn't choose, or they allow other people to convince them to travel unfamiliar roads. There may even be times when someone convinces *you* to travel a road with them and somewhere along the way they no longer want to travel with you, or you realize that the road you are traveling is dangerous and uncertain. If you stop and pay attention, you will see the signs that tell you to avoid these journey partners or steer clear of untraveled roads.

Here are a few tips for savoring the messages of the valley and getting to the mountaintop:

- Know that you are in the valley for a reason. The key is to figure out why.

- Know that there is a message in the reason. What is the message? What are you suppose to learn in the valley?

- Did someone help or cause you to get in the valley? Who are the people around you who have taken you off your path? Do you have to have them in your life?

- Are you in the valley often? Why do you keep ending up here? What do you need to change?

Delicious!

If you find yourself in a valley, know that it is not your destiny to be there for long. There may be a specific lesson you need to learn in the valley. You may be in the valley so that you can be alone in your thoughts to really reflect on the direction of your life. You may be in the valley because you needed something drastic to wake you up and make you pay attention to what is going on in your life.

We all will have valleys in our lives, but we do not have to stay there any longer than we choose.

29

Delicious Living Tip #3

A savvy woman knows when she is in the valley, and she uses her internal tools to climb to the mountaintop. What internal tools do you have for the climb?

Food for Thought

What ingredients did you extract from this chapter to create your own recipe for a delicious life? Use the space below to record your thoughts.

Delicious!

Chapter 4
Get Out of Your Own Way

Intention is when are fully awakened in each moment, do things with a sense of purpose, and deliberately live your life on your own terms…

Being intentional means taking charge of your life and living on purpose.

Are you worried, complaining, and feeling sorry for yourself or maybe wishing, hoping, and praying that your dreams will come true? Many people sit and wait for the sky to open up with an undeniable message that will hit them in the head like a brick. You were chosen to be on this earth for a reason—a divine reason—but you may not know exactly what the reason is. Some folks go through life breathing and taking up space without truly living out their divine purpose in life.

I believe a power greater than ourselves lives in each of us and speaks not only in that quiet voice called intuition but boldly, like the brick that hits us in the head with tremendous force. We know when the brick hits us, but we ignore or do not know how to listen and respond to that quiet, divine voice inside.

My experience tells me that 90 percent of the time that divine voice comes through a quiet channel that we fail to hear if we are not intentionally and actively seeking to hear its subtle message. I have encountered many people, mostly women, who have no idea what they are here on earth to do. They are unhappy, confused, angry, and filled with the lethal fluid of "settling for life as it is." This is manifested through staying in the rocking chair of life, working at a job you hate, complaining about your current circumstances, holding on to the past, failing to create movement in your life, or blaming everybody else for the status of your life.

People like this are stuck in survival mode. They live one day at a time, spinning their wheels and never getting ahead. The divine power that I believe in does not want this type of life for you. So how do you go from surviving to thriving?

To thrive is to flourish and blossom, to become successful and prosperous. It has been said for decades that one must truly get sick and tired of being sick and tired before any change can happen in one's life. If you have not hit rock bottom yet, you may continue to complain, worry, and blame. If you are truly tired of surviving and want to thrive, then get out your pen and paper and take note of the fundamentals of living a life of abundance. You don't have to wait for the "change gonna come," because you are the creator of your reality and you are the one who is responsible for your life.

Walk by faith. That means move; don't stand still. You must take one step at a time and move forward every day. Joy is waiting for you to peel away the layers of gloom

Delicious!

and doom so it can be luminous in your life… so you can live a delicious life.

Change is constant and fluid if you allow the natural course of evolution to take place. I believe we have the power to increase the intensity, direction, and speed of change if we choose to do so, and if we do it with awareness and intent. My hope is that if you were sitting still or feeling stuck before you began to read this book, you have gotten up from the couch, the pity-pot, or a place of darkness and said, "No more!, I am going to begin living my life!" If you are still waiting for the brick to hit you, stop waiting. If you have tuned into your inner voice, listen closely…

Not all messages come to us clearly and distinctly. We must master the art of summoning our inner voice and be able to hear it at its faintest vibration. If you struggle with controlling your thoughts, you might find it more helpful to learn how to begin paying attention to your emotions and feelings. Have you ever thought of doing something but your gut (inner self or inner voice) said, "No, don't do that; it's not a good idea"? You might have even experienced or felt a sense of fear, danger, or apprehension as this thought occurred to you. That message came from the voice that truly guides your thoughts and actions. You must become aware of that voice so that you can begin using it as a guide to creating your delicious life.

To act with intention means to do something with a sense of purpose, a plan, or a goal. An intentional action has meaning. Many people get up and go through their daily routines without intention, operating on auto-pilot. They get in the shower, wash up, dry off, and continue their grooming routine. When was the last time you paid attention to how the warm water felt as it ran down your body? When was the last time you deeply inhaled the scent of your body wash and relished the aroma? When was the last time you felt every wipe of the washcloth as you cleansed your skin? It's easy to just hop in the shower and think of all the things on your to-do list, then to get out and miss the true experience of a nice, hot, refreshing shower. That's how many people go through life.

When you think, live, and act with intention, you utilize all of your senses to entirely experience each moment. When you operate on auto-pilot you are not able to savor the luscious flavor of living. It is difficult to create the life you want if you function each day on cruise control. You must be present and fully awake in every moment. It is time to wake up and take control of your life and stop letting other people and events construct your destiny. Remember that when you give energy to something, it grows abundantly in your life. This will happen even if it's not something you want, so be careful to devote your mental, emotional, and spiritual energy to the things you need, want, and desire.

Here are five tips for living a life of awareness and intention:

1. Think of the three most important people in your life. They might include your child, parent, spouse, partner, or friend. Close your eyes and think about how it feels to be in the presence of each person. When you envision being with each person, do you feel joy, peace, or happiness? If not, that is a sign that your relationship with them is out of synch and not in alignment with the desires of your soul.

2. When you engage with strangers, co-workers, your boss, and other people, pay attention to how you feel when you are in their presence. If you do not feel positive sensations or feelings, you must become aware

Delicious!

of this disconnect and intentionally decide who you will choose to share space with. It's your decision.

3. For one full day, pay attention to your surroundings by using all of your senses to take in the information from the environment. What do you see, hear, smell, taste, and feel when you are at work, home, church, school, and every other setting and moment you experience?

4. For one full day, make decisions based on what feels right. Choose a course of action based only on if it is likely to change your life for the better. In other words, if the outcome of your decision is going to change the direction of your life and or take you to the next level, then do it; if not, maybe you should do something different.

5. If you know your purpose in life, do something every day that will help you to reach your goals or live your purpose. If you do not know your purpose, ask yourself this question: "If I had unlimited money and no worries, what would I do for free? How would I love to spend my days?" If you can't find an answer to this question immediately, ask yourself again each day until the answer is clear beyond a doubt.

Again, we all are here for a delicious reason. It is critical that you determine what makes you feel alive. What makes you feel happy inside? You must determine the one thing that you could not imagine NOT doing in this lifetime. Once you figure it out, hold on to it, nourish it, protect it, and grow it every day. Remember to listen to your inner voice; the faint yet powerful voice of your soul; it's waiting to speak loudly in your life.

If you desire to be successful in creating a delicious life, you must get out of your own way. Yes, that's right:

YOU are the biggest obstacle standing in the way of more vibrant living. How do I know? I, too, have been in my own way, and from time to time I get in my own way still. The great thing is that I have learned to know when I am getting in my own way and immediately move, shift, and reposition myself to allow the power and abundance of the universe to begin moving in my life.

Don't make things more complicated than they need to be. What if I told you there are only five things you need to do every day to live a deliciously vibrant life? Could it be that easy? Of course it can! Here they are; don't question them, just do it!

Five daily actions for vibrant living:

1. If you wake up loving yourself, faults and all, you have already won half the battle.

2. If you give back to the world unselfishly, everything you desire will come back to you tenfold. Live to give.

3. If you show gratitude, the universe will bless you more abundantly, and if you live on purpose your provisions will be met (that includes your needs, wants and desires).

4. If you intentionally walk out your destiny through faith and take baby steps in the right direction, you will create a sweet, vibrant life.

5. If you face your fears, learn from your mistakes, and stay out of your own way, the life you desire will come with ease and grace.

Quite simply, you have two choices: allow your challenges to keep you stuck in life, or embrace them, look

Delicious!

for the lesson in each life challenge, and use the lesson to change the direction of your life.

You are the creator of your destiny. Stop wasting your time trying to gain the approval of others. Define your life and live it deliciously on your own terms. Do what you love every day! I realize these simple actions may seem more difficult than they should be, but just try it. Simply stop looking, searching, pulling, begging, asking, and fumbling through life and just BE you.

While coaching and counseling many clients, I've realized there are five main reasons people are unfulfilled in their lives. These five reasons are perfect examples of how you may be holding yourself back from living a delicious life. See if any of these apply to your life right now.

Five habits that could be holding you back:

- *Counterproductive thinking:* Giving thought energy to things that don't matter.

- *Negative thinking:* Telling yourself "This is impossible; it will never work."

- *Dwelling on the past:* Shoulda, coulda, woulda. "Why did do this instead of that?"

- *Fear-filled thinking:* "I don't have enough money, what if I fail, what will people say, I can't, I shouldn't, I would, but…"

- *Entertaining the internal critic:* Listening to it, believing it, and giving it power.

As you can see, these obstacles are all anchored in your thoughts. Therefore, creating a delicious life begins in your mind. I've always believed your thoughts determine your feelings, your feelings determine your actions and behavior, and your behavior determines how you live your life. So, as you look around and reflect upon how you are living and who you are, you will see that your life is the direct result of your thoughts. In one way or another, you have thought your way to your current circumstances. The wonderful news is that you can also think you way to new and more delicious circumstances. You can use your thoughts to create the life you love.

Here are a few strategies to help you begin thinking your way to a delicious life:

- Choose positive, action-oriented words to describe yourself and your intentions: "I *am*, I *have*, I *can*..."

- Talk yourself into action instead of talking yourself out of action. Tell yourself all the reasons why you *should* do something instead of why not.

- Learn to recognize and avoid the gateways to getting sucked into other people's dramas. For example, they may start a conversation with phrases like these: "Today was awful, I am so pissed right now, you wouldn't believe what happened to me today..." (It's important not to allow potentially negative conversations to steal your mental, emotional, or spiritual energy.)

If your thoughts are filled with "shoulda, coulda, woulda" or "why did or didn't I," you can be sure that those messages are not coming from your higher self. So if you have to make a decision about something, get quiet and still. Wait for the message that feels right—one you are drawn to and one that gives you the sense that "all is well." Stop wrestling with your thoughts; allow your higher self to be your guide not only in thoughts and decisions but throughout life in general. To be successful at changing your thoughts, you must become very intentional (purposeful and deliberate).

If you can take one nugget from this chapter and start applying it right now, I would recommend that you create intentions for your life, intentions for how you want to be, intentions for how you want to live and show up in the world. A delicious life won't fall out of the sky; you have to intentionally create it every day.

Intentions are like positive affirmations. You state them in the present tense. They are based on something you want or desire greatly. When you say your intention statements out loud, you broadcast an energy message into the universe and the universe responds. Be careful what you focus on, because if you focus on things that you don't want, that is exactly what you will get even if you never say it out loud. So if you are thinking, for example, "I hate my job," you will continue to work in a job you hate. If you think "My mate does not appreciate me" you will continue to look for and receive unappreciative behavior. So make sure you focus your mental energy on what you *want and desire* all the time.

Instead of focusing your energy on a job you don't like, say something like this: "I am excited about the possibility of finding a job I love." You can create intention statements for various areas of your life or create one that encapsulates your mantra for living. On the next page are a few intention statements you can use, or you can create your own.

The key to using an intention statement is to mean it when you say it. You must believe it can happen, and you must feel it deeply when you think or say it. The final step is to fully accept that the statement applies to you and in the meantime carry out intentional behaviors that will speed up the manifestation process.

Now you have received several strategies to begin creating your life on your own terms. To recap, here is what you should do: (1) Define *delicious* and *radiant* in your own way, creating a definition you choose to live by; (2) Begin taking back your life from all the things and people that keep you from living a delicious life; (3) Learn from the valley moments in life, but don't stay in the valley; instead, take baby steps toward your destiny; (4) Get out of your own way and begin living the life you desire. The ability to do all of those things requires you to face your fears head-on and courageously conquer the things that have kept you captive in a bland life.

Delicious!

Food for Thought

What ingredients did you extract from this chapter to create your own recipe for a delicious life? Use the space below to record your thoughts.

Delicious!

Chapter 5
A Delicious Life Does Not Include Excuses

Willingness is the ability to stretch your imagination beyond belief and to be open to new possibilities...

Free your mind from doubts that hold you hostage.

43

I have made a lot of excuses in my life: excuses not to do something, go somewhere, or become the person I knew I could become. Today there is no room for excuses. There is no room for mediocrity... no room to settle for less than I deserve. I'll bet you've made similar excuses. Maybe you've talked yourself out of doing things that could dramatically change your life for the better. You may have talked yourself out of an opportunity or moment that could open magical doors to your destiny. I have learned that usually this happens because we are afraid to fail or may even fear success. I also realize there are people who make excuses because they are lazy, unmotivated, or fail to take responsibility for their lives.

More often than not, excuses come from a foundation of fear. Fear is like kryptonite. It paralyzes, hinders, weakens, and stops you in your tracks. Fear causes you to remain in the "rocking chair" of life, moving without going anywhere. Fear causes you to remain blind to your full potential and to stay captive in a life that lacks brilliance, vibrancy, and luminosity. Fear keeps the gray clouds forever hovering over your life, and thus you live with more days of potential rain than days of sunshine. Today, right now in this moment, you will declare more sunshine in your life. If you seek to live a deliciously vibrant life, you must do two things: stop making excuses about your life and face your fears. What happens if you don't? You will remain stuck, immobilized, and years from now you will still be sitting in the same old rocking chair of life, making a lot of movement but getting nowhere. I'd like to share with you the most common excuses made by people who are living in fear, along a strategy to help you begin to move beyond that particular excuse.

Excuse #1: "I don't have time."

Sometimes it appears there are not enough hours in the day to meet the demands of life. I am fairly confident that if you were told you had only one week to live, you would find time to do the things that are on your personal lifetime "to do" list because they really matter to you.

In essence, when you use this excuse you are saying that you are not important or you do not deserve to get what you want, become who you desire, go where you want to go, and live how you want to live. My dear sister friend, you DO deserve it, whatever it may be. Please stop procrastinating in your life. Get out of the rocking chair and get moving. Don't wait! Live your life like you only have a week to live, and do it with passion, purpose, and intention.

Delicious!

Excuse #2: "I can't afford it."

I've used this one many times myself and have come to realize that this excuse boils down to two things. You either believe you are not worthy of whatever it is you can't afford, or you are operating from a "lacking" mentality. A lacking mentality means you are holding on to money just in case you need it or just in case something happens and maybe even because you fear if you spend the money on this thing or object you cannot afford you will be lacking money when you need it for something more important. While this may have an element of truth, the silent message you are sending out into the universe is "Money prevents me from having what I want or need, and my feelings about money are ruling how I make decisions in my life." If this sounds like you, try using the following intention statement when you begin to fret about whether to spend money: "Money comes and goes easily and abundantly in my life."

Saying and believing in this intention statement moves you from a place of lack to a place of abundance. It allows you to trust that all is well despite the amount of money you have, and to feel secure in the knowledge that your provisions will be met if you trust and believe they will.

I use this intention statement every day, and it has helped tremendously in reducing my fear about not having enough money. When I first started my business full-time about two years ago I was constantly worried about money even when I didn't think I was. My body expressed this worry in the form of tension, body aches, headaches, and restless sleeping. Don't fool yourself; your body will communicate to you when something is out of whack mentally, emotionally, or spiritually. That's why you must master the art of being intentionally awake in every moment so you will know when things are not in alignment. (In other words, wake up and pay attention!)

Excuse #3: "I don't know how."

You may use this excuse because you really don't know how to do something or because you don't want to learn how. There are many things I don't know how to do, but if it is something I really want to learn how to do, the excuse of "I don't know how" quickly goes out the window. If you use this excuse to avoid doing something that could change your life, you are ultimately saying you don't want to change your life.

When you find yourself using this excuse, ask yourself the following questions: "Do I want to learn how?" or "How can I learn how to do this?" If you want to create a life you love, you must stop using this as an excuse and figure out how to do what you want to do. It's that simple: either choose to remain ignorant and fearful, or make a decision to take responsibility for your life and allow yourself to be open to learning new ways of creating the life you desire.

Simply, making excuses is more about fear than about laziness. Do not let your fears keep you from doing what you want to do, going where you want to go, getting what you want, and most importantly being who you want to become. From this day forth, I challenge you to begin talking yourself *into* doing the things you know will make your life more delicious, rather than talking yourself out of them.

To live a delicious life, you must actively be engaged in your life. Delicious living requires an intentional series of daily actions that take your life to another level, often revealing the authentic you with each act. Don't let life pass you by. Stop making excuses right now. Savvy women know that excuses are intentional reasons to fail. Savvy women know what ingredients are required to create a sweet and savory life.

Delicious Living Tip #5

Savvy women make it happen, no matter what circumstances they are in. Do something each day to re-invent yourself. Begin each morning with this thought: "How can I become better today than I was yesterday?" and then do it! The intention is to peel away layers of the old you to reveal a new and more vibrant you...

Food for Thought

What ingredients did you extract from this chapter to create your own recipe for a delicious life? Use the space below to record your thoughts.

Delicious!

Chapter 6
Stare Fear in the Face and Say "Bring It On"

Courage is doing what you know is right and challenging at the same time…

Courage: valor, daring, audacity, determination, strength.

Fear speaks to us in a variety of ways. It talks to our spirit and chatters away in our minds. Fear's conversation ultimately is always the same. Fear speaks words of doubt, apprehension, and often results in lack of action or procrastination.

When you live in fear, you think or say things that keep you from discovering your full potential. When you live in fear, you think or say things like "I can't," "I don't have enough money," "I will get myself straight when my finances are in order," "I'll do it when the kids get a little older" and "I can't because other things and people are more important."

The language of fear causes you to worry about things you have no control over or things that are not relevant to your life. The language of fear creates confusion about how to begin living your life with passion. Fear keeps you in contemplation mode, making you unsure of what to do with your life. When you listen to the language of fear, you procrastinate both in your personal and professional life by doubting your ability, not believing in yourself, and second-guessing your decisions.

The language of fear is powerful beyond measure. Some people are not fully aware that the chattering in their mind is fear-driven and purposeful. I like to call this chattering your life tapes; often these tapes are old, exaggerated, and based on previous life experiences.

What are your mental tapes saying to you?

When fear mentally and emotionally shows up in your life it causes you to think and behave in certain ways. Below are the most common manifestations of fear. How many of these are evident in your life?

Immobilization—You remain in transition, stuck in one place and going nowhere.

Denial—You make comments like "Things will get better" or "It's not so bad."

Procrastination—You start things and rarely finish them.

Confusion—You are unclear about your life and often think or say "I don't know what to do."

Lethargy—You are emotionally and physically tired most of the time.

Emotional numbness—You have an "I don't care" attitude and rarely express true emotion.

Doubt—You have difficulty believing in yourself and think "I will never be able to change my life."

Blame—You fail to take responsibility for your life and often use phrases such as "If everyone else would" or "I could have if done it if so and so would have…"

Avoidance—You don't face issues head-on, and you say things like "I'll do it tomorrow."

Delicious!

There is hope in facing fear. People have accomplished great things and overcome great obstacles in the midst of fear. Think about a mother who miraculously rescues her child from a wild animal or lifts up a car that is on top of someone she loves. Fear motivates her to reach deep inside and find extraordinary strength and courage to defy the odds. You have that same strength and courage inside of you. That thought alone is scary. Some people don't fear failure; in fact, they fear success. This is not uncommon. Being successful demands that people are credible, wise, strong, accountable, and responsible. Some people are afraid that they may not be able to live up to these standards. They may even fear they will lose friends or gain new friends they are unsure how to engage with.

I challenge you to begin facing your fears. Begin to see fear as the fuel that can ignite your life. Let your fears drive you toward your passion and purpose and master the *art of fear-free living!*

Defining Fear

Fear can be described as dread, terror, panic, apprehension, worry, or fright. Fear is one of the most immobilizing emotions of the human spirit. Fear can keep you stuck emotionally, mentally, and spiritually regardless of the source and intensity of your fears. Fear keeps your life in a holding pattern; similar to that of an airplane hovering above the airport waiting to land. The plane can only hover so long before it will have to either attempt to land or spiral downward into destruction. On the other hand, fear can have positive implications if you are able to see the silver lining. Fear can move you into action and move you from flight mode into fight mode. Fear can also cause you to become awakened into action and face the challenges before you. Fear can be the motivating factor that causes you to finally realize that enough is enough. Regardless of the source of fear, you have the choice to either succumb to or face your fears. Failure to do so has serious implications to be considered as you contemplate your plan of action.

Trust yourself. You'll know what fear looks and feels like if you pay attention to how your body responds to certain people and situations. Listen to that inner voice...

What does fear look like?

Fear has extreme power in our lives, and this is what it looks like in real life. Fear may cause you to:

- Put up with an overbearing boss.
- Stay at a job you hate.
- Remain in a relationship that is unhealthy.
- Allow your children to run the house.
- Never write the book in your heart.
- Let your family and friends dictate your life.
- Listen to the negative messages in your mind.
- Not ask for the raise you know you deserve.
- Keep your dreams a secret.
- Not take personal and professional risks.
- Fail to confront the people who are making your life miserable.
- Avoid networking opportunities.
- Procrastinate on creating the life you desire.
- Stay stuck in a place of discontent and apathy.

Does this sound like you or your life? If so, what are you waiting for?

Delicious!

When fear mentally and emotionally shows up in your life it causes you to think and behave in certain ways. When you live in fear, you have a heightened sense of awareness, you are on guard and ready, you may move into fight or flight mode, you seek to self-preserve and may become emotionally energized. I hope that you will get sick and tired of living in fear and do something to change your life.

The manifestations of fear can be a good thing if you choose to see and use them that way. Awareness allows you to see what is present or missing. To bring about change, you must wake up from the fog of denial and see what is in front of and behind you.

Being on guard means you are prepared for action. You are positioned to take action. You must be ready at any moment to face not only your fears but other unexpected life challenges. Quick decisions may sound hasty but when fear arises unexpectedly you have to be ready for combat. Yes, you have to be ready to fight for your emotional and spiritual survival. You only have one life to live. Being in fight mode simply means you refuse to lie down and let fear run your life. Fight mode is the opposite of flight mode; it means you are ready to face your fears instead of ignoring them and hoping they will go away on their own.

Self-preservation simply means eat or die. If you don't nourish your body, you will become sick and eventually die. The same thing is true about the importance of feeding your soul. Fear keeps you from digesting the sweetness of life. The sweetness of life includes things like peace, happiness, and abundance. You must begin to see the significance of feeding your soul just as you feed your body.

Having significant emotional energy to sustain life is essential. When you run out of gas, you stop functioning. You must be very protective of your emotional energy and refuse to let people suck you dry. You must begin to identify the joy stealers in your life. These are people who are miserable, angry, and jealous. These people will invade your emotional gas tank and siphon out all of your reserves, leaving you immobilized. Being emotionally energized means you preserve your energy and function in life with passion and vitality. It is also important to have several energy stations available to refuel your spirit. These would be people who support you, believe in you, and act as coaches, mentors, cheerleaders, and most importantly genuine friends.

When you get sick and tired of being sick and tired, you most often will fight back. Fighting back is not a bad thing; in fact, it is sometimes necessary. We must strive for more than survival and seek to be individuals who thrive in all facets of our lives. When you get sick and tired you stand up for yourself and begin to assert and voice your needs and desires. Some people have to reach this stage before they take action. Despite what stage you reach it is your right to be free of the things that bind you.

Living fear-free is an art, because each of us defines fear on her own terms and fear affects each of us differently. It is an art because fear and its manifestations can often be abstract, and only we know the true meaning behind the images on our canvas of life. If I asked ten people to draw what fear looks life in their life, there would be ten different portraits with ten different meanings.

The way we as individuals live our life is an art in itself, and therefore living fear-free is an artistic representation of ourselves and how we choose to live. In this moment, I am

Delicious!

giving you permission to be aware, on guard, and energized to begin the necessary life task of self-preservation. Are you ready to create your new life? First examine the next steps.

Catriceology's Simple Steps for Conquering Your Fears

1. Clearly define your fears. Determine the source. Are they real or imagined? How much distress are they causing in your life? How is the distress creating negativity in your life?

2. Ask yourself this question: "What's the worst thing that could happen if I do not face my fears?" This is an important step. Sometimes people blow their fears out of proportion. I suggest you literally write down each fear and compare the consequences of facing or ignoring your fears.

3. Realize that you have a choice: either face your fears or live in fear. Yes, it really is that simple. It is as simple as eat or die. I realize that facing your fears is a task that requires emotional strength, courage, daily intentional behavior, and a support system. You can do it if you choose. Great or sought-after things in life do not come easily.

To help you conquer you fears, here are five simple tools to begin drafting a fear-free life. I hope you will take these tools and use them to create a life of clarity, purpose, peace, and abundance. In conjunction with my tools, you will need a few tools of your own: courage, honesty, and perseverance.

Tools for Creating Your Fear-Free Life

1. **A new canvas:** Your mind is the canvas of life. If you think it and believe it; you can do it and have it regardless of what "it" happens to be. Today take down the old canvas and put up a new and clear canvas to begin creating the life you want.

2. **A colorful paint set:** Having supportive people in your life is essential. I encourage you to get rid of the gray and dull people who cast clouds over your life. Choose to have colorful, happy, and energetic people in your life today. These people will fill your canvas with joy, laughter, and most importantly, their belief in you.

3. **A big eraser:** Life is full of opportunities, and as you seek them you will be apprehensive and even make mistakes along the way. Successful people take action and they don't see mistakes as failure but rather opportunities for growth. Go ahead and use this big eraser to erase the negative thoughts about yourself. Erase the past hurts that are keeping you stuck. Erase everything in your life that is causing you distress and misery.

4. **A bright light:** Painting and creating in the dark is not optimal. The light of your life can be whatever you determine it to be. If it is God, then use his power and grace to keep you focused on your goals. If it's your children, let them be the reminder you need to craft the life you desire. Use something outside yourself as your motivation to take action, and draw energy from that source every day.

5. **A sturdy easel:** While you are creating your fear-free life you are going to need support. You will need something strong to hold in place the canvas of your

Delicious!

life. Take inventory of all the things that give you strength, and rely on these people, actions, or events as your foundation for facing your fears.

As you begin to create a fear-free life, remember that you have the tools you need within you; you just have to seek them and use them.

Using Intentional Behaviors to Conquer Your Fears

Intentional behaviors are mental, physical, and emotional acts that you "do" with a motive or purpose. Many of us go through life on auto-pilot and work from a habitual routine without thinking about what we are doing and why we are doing it.

Beginning today, I want you to begin making everything you say, think, and do intentional. When you use intentional behavior, you are "creating" the life you want. Stop living in "habit" mode. Do things that will profit you in the end. Do things that are specifically meant to create a new life. Do things that will move you one step closer to your life goals.

Below are a few examples of intentional behavior. The only way to conquer your fears is to identify them and face them relentlessly.

- Make a list of all your fears. Put the list in a place that will see each day, do something daily to face your fears. Write each fear on a small slip of paper and put them in a small paper lunch bag. Each day pull out a fear and commit to doing something to begin facing and conquering it. If you face it, throw it away the slip of paper; if not, put it back in the bag. Do this until each fear is gone.

- Identify all of the people who create stress, pain, misery, and negativity in your life. Start paying attention to how you feel when these people are in your presence. These are the people who give you all the reasons you can't or shouldn't do something you want to do. These are the people whose presence gives you a headache, upset stomach, or feelings of annoyance. These are the people who, when you see them coming, you wish you could run the other way. These are the people who, when you finish talking to them, leave you with feelings of being overwhelmed and emotionally drained. Once you have identified them, you have to make a decision. Here are some options: (1) Tell them how they make you feel in the hope that they will change their behavior. (2) Decide to not engage with them in order to protect your energy source. (3) Deal with them in a superficial way by distancing yourself as much as possible. The choice is yours. Decide based upon the necessity and quality of the relationship, but remember that you do have a choice!

Facing your fears can be scary and daunting. You really have two choices: either face your fears or live in fear. If you choose to live in fear, then you must take full responsibility for the outcomes associated with living in fear. This means you can blame only yourself for the quality and direction of your life. Facing your fears is simply about taking risks. This means that you may risk losing your job, losing friends and family bonds, risk losing an identity, and the list goes on and on. On the next page are some very specific questions to ask yourself about taking the risk to face your fears.

Delicious!

- What do I need to face? What am I afraid of facing or doing? (Identify the fear.)

- What do I stand to gain or lose by facing this fear? (Potential danger or benefit)

- What is the likelihood of that gain being realized? (Can I see or visualize the benefit?)

- Do past experiences and common sense indicate that the odds are in my favor? (What risks have I taken in the past, and what were the outcomes?)

- How much would I lose if I took this risk and it failed totally? (What's the worst thing that could happen?)

- How much am I willing to put on the line? (How much vulnerability am I willing to expose?)

- How much will I gain? (How will facing this fear improve my own life or the lives of the people I love?)

Is there something you really want to do, but you are afraid to jump in, take the leap, or face the unknown? Fear can be immobilizing and cause us to question our abilities, thoughts, and decisions. When you let fear keep you stuck, you internally stand still and your life seems never to move forward, leaving you unsatisfied.

Are you contemplating getting a new job or quitting your job? What is the worst thing that can happen if you do? Are you considering starting a new business or becoming an entrepreneur? What will happen to your spirit/soul if you don't? Are you thinking about leaving an unhealthy relationship? If you stay, how much damage are you causing to your spirit and the spirits of your children? Stop thinking about what will happen if you leave; instead, focus on what will happen if you don't!

If you did not wake up tomorrow morning, would you have lived the life you desire? Have you loved people deeply? Have you spent as much time with your children as you desire? Are you doing what you love?

Stop right now and answer the following questions:

1. Determine the reason you exist. Why are you here on this earth? Make your answer clear and specific, and write it down.

2. Determine your deepest desire. What do you really want to be doing with your life? Write it down, and take steps every day to live your passion.

Delicious!

3. Determine what is holding you back. Who or what is keeping you stuck and unfulfilled? Make a plan to remove this influence from your life.

4. Determine what your gifts are. What can you do that no one else can do? What natural gifts can you share with the world? Discover them and give back to the world. Start with the people closest to you. When you give unselfishly, you receive abundantly.

5. Stop complaining, worrying, contemplating, overanalyzing, and hesitating about your life. You have only one life to live. What things are you worrying about or contemplating right now?

6. Determine your life goals. Make a list of things you want to do before you die. These can be simple things or extravagant things. Now begin doing them instead of dreaming about them. Each time you accomplish one of your life goals, cross it off and move on to the next one.

Chapter 6: Stare Fear in the Face and Say "Bring It On"

My life goals:

Fear can dramatically affect your spirit. Fear keeps your authentic spirit captive and prevents you from being vibrant every day, in every moment.

1. Who or what is blocking your prosperity?

2. Who or what has control over your life?

3. What can you give back to the world to keep the flow of receiving in movement?

4. Are you living on purpose and doing what you love every day?

Delicious!

5. Are you working toward becoming your highest self?

When you have successfully answered the questions and carried out the exercises in this chapter, you will have begun the process of living a fear-free life. When you can stare your fear in the face, say "bring it on," and create your delicious life despite your fears, you will have mastered the *art of fear-free living!* Do it afraid, my sisterfriend, do it afraid...

Delicious Living Tip #6
A savvy woman is clear about her fears and determined to conquer them. If fear causes you to become stuck or to move slowly, check your spirit to see what you are afraid of...

Food for Thought

What ingredients did you extract from this chapter to create your own recipe for a delicious life? Use the space below to record your thoughts.

Delicious!

Chapter 7
Girlfriend, Just BE Delicious!

Satisfaction is when you can look in the mirror and love everything you see, including your limitations...

Satisfied: contented, pleased, comfortable, at ease, happy!

Do you have a clear vision for your life? I mean, specific and crystal-clear? This is so important as you begin to release your juicy goodness—your deliciousness—and reveal it to the world. Many times people are unclear and unfocused, yet they expect their dreams to come true. I've learned the significance of keeping things simple and clear.

You may not know every step needed to manifest your dreams, but having a clear picture of how you want to BE will let you take baby steps toward creating that reality. I encourage you to shift your focus from what you want to *become, have,* or *do* and instead put the emphasis on how you want to BE, in this moment, in every moment. *Being* affords you more peace, ease and grace. *Becoming* causes doubt, worry, and stress. Shift your focus toward *being* the person you want to be in each moment, and in time you will *become* that person.

One of the greatest lessons I have learned in the past year is that even though you may not be able to control the things going on in your life, you surely have control over how you respond to them. You can choose in every moment to either re-act or act. I have found that "acting" is much more productive. When you re-act you give into the problem, allowing it to consume you and deplete your emotional energy. You need your emotional energy to fully manifest your heart's desires, so protect it, nurture it, and preserve it.

By the way, do you know what your heart's desires are? Have you slowed down enough to really discover the hidden treasures within? If you could wake up tomorrow and find yourself doing what you want, living how you want to live, or being who you want to be, what would that look like? The picture must be crystal-clear before you can begin to manifest it. Go ahead—create a delicious vision!

Here are some questions to help you create a crystal-clear vision of your delicious life:

1. Where do you live?
2. Who is with you?
3. How much money do you make?
4. How do you spend your time?
5. What kind of house do you live in?
6. What kind of car do you drive?
7. What do you do for relaxation?
8. How are you giving back to the world?
9. How do you feel on the inside?
10. How are you showing up in the world?
11. What do you stand for?
12. How are you living out your core values?
13. What makes you happy, alive, and joyful?
14. How are you loving the skin you are in?
15. How, exactly, are you enjoying each day of your life?

Delicious!

Get clear, specific, focused, and intentional about how you want to live and be. Do something every day to take yourself one step closer to your dream life. Once you know what you want and the vision is clear, just do it. That's right—take intentional steps toward creating a life you love. During the process, don't push, beg, pull, force, and struggle. If you begin to struggle through this process, that is a sign that you are moving in the wrong direction. When you are living on purpose and walking out your destiny, for the most part it should feel right and done with ease. Yes, of course there will be bumps in the road, but you should be able to quickly navigate through those moments when you use your soul as a compass. When you master the art of "being," you don't have to chase things and struggle through life. When you are living on purpose things will happen, people will show up, doors will open, coincidences will happen, and what you desire will come to you when you least expect it. Sisterfriend, please stop struggling in your life; just wake up, love the skin you're in, and be delicious!

This poem is for all my sisters who just want to be ...

Just Be... A soul poem by Catrice M. Jackson

Have you ever found moments where you can just BE?
Hmmmmm, so sweet. I love it when I can just BE...
No worries, no masks, not a care in the world, just ME!
Why doesn't life allow you to just BE?
Life does—it's people who want to see you in misery...
I love being me—free, bold, happy, and content—just peacefully me!
I seek to have more of those days of just being me.
The days where I wake up and look in the mirror and love what I see.

Chapter 7: Girlfriend, Just BE Delicious!

Those moments where I step into the world sure of my intentions and integrity…

Being me make me feel alive inside.

Being me feels natural—I'm filled with pride.

You see, being me is who I am designed to be.

Being me is not dictated by what *you* want or what *they* want but rather what *I* want.

You see…being me allows my spirit to be free.

Being me produces my creativity, and my creativity is what keeps me alive—inside.

I need to be free—free from the drama, the expectations, the lies and the excuses… the false promises and phony, superficial smiles and hellos of those who mean me no good.

Free is the only way for me to be me. I refuse to be captive to other people's egos, perspectives, and expectations of me.

68

Girl… take my advice: stop fighting it, quit worrying about it, do what you do, be who you be, love who you love, dream how you wanna dream, and by the way… don't let *nobody* make you feel inferior. Humph! If you know like I know, you better just be!

Be strong!
Be bold!
Be joyful!

Be delicious!
Be FREE—oh, my sister, please just be…

A Soul Poem by Catrice Jackson © 2009.

Delicious!

Chapter 7: Girlfriend, Just BE Delicious!

Food for Thought

What ingredients did you extract from this chapter to create your own recipe for a delicious life? Use the space below to record your thoughts.

Delicious!

Chapter 8
Love the Skin You Are In

Love is accepting that you are an imperfect woman and still embracing and appreciating every part of who you are...

Love: adore, admire, appreciate, cherish, respect.

If we slow down and take notice of the simple yet wonderful things in life, we will soon realize that we already have all we need. Living a delicious life means waking up feeling grateful and *knowing* that everything is going to be okay. Living deliciously allows you to live on purpose and know your provisions will be met so you can go through the day with no worries or fear. Living deliciously allows you to stop struggling, pushing, begging, forcing, and trying to be in control of every little thing.

A delicious life is your destiny. It is the way God intended your life to be. An essential step in living a delicious life is simply to love the skin you are in. If you can just love the skin you're in and be grateful for what you have, you can be assured that everything else you need and want will be given to you in abundance.

There is great liberation and freedom in loving yourself fully. It allows you to be in the moment without worrying what other people think of you. When you can do this, you are able to experience a full awakening of your mind, body, and spirit. Use this affirmation to help you become mindful of the importance of loving the skin you are in. "I will stop making life so complicated and create the delicious life I desire and deserve through simple actions."

Self-love,,,,

Some would say *self-love* is vain and some would say it's not Godlike, but others would say it's essential for living a purposeful life and being able to give love back to the world. I believe the old saying is true: if you don't love yourself, how can you love others? I've encountered many people who either don't know how to love themselves or are afraid they are unworthy of any kind of love, including loving themselves. I also believe that you must love yourself in order to live fully in the world. Self-love is not an impossible thing to do; in fact, you can choose to do so right now, in this moment.

Self-love is essential in developing lasting relationships, discovering your passion, living on purpose, loving what you do in life and career, and attracting the desires of your heart. If you are seeking more peace, clarity, and luminosity in life, begin with self... loving yourself exactly how you are. If you seek to become your highest, most prosperous self, learn how to be in love with yourself—yes, there is a difference; do you know why? Reflect back on the last time you were deeply in love with someone. If you remember, you probably couldn't wait to see them, the sound of their name brought joy to your heart, you would do almost anything to make them happy, and the list goes on and on. Why shouldn't you feel the same way about yourself? When you are in love you are focused on the relationship, you take extra special time and care grooming yourself, you feel alive inside and can't wait to be with the person you are in love with. I want you to start today learning how to fall back in love with yourself. This means to begin doing all the things you would normally do for the person you are in love with and start doing these special things for yourself. I want you to get excited about the time you will spend alone with yourself. I want you to do almost anything (within reason) to make yourself happy. I want you to take extra care and time caring for and pampering yourself. Most importantly, I want you to become *intensely* focused on YOU, how you want to BE and how you want to live your life. As you begin the journey of self-love you will have to sit down, get quiet, and take inventory of who you are, faults and all. I want you to capitalize on your strengths by making them stronger. I want you to accept your limitations and work on minimizing or eliminating them.

You must reflect upon how well or not so well you are taking care of yourself and whether you are giving special attention to your emotional, physical, mental, and spiritual needs and wants. It's time to stop putting yourself last. It's time to stop treating everybody else better than you treat yourself. It's time to stop focusing on everyone else's faults and work on becoming *your* best self.

"The greatest magnifying glasses in the world are a man's own eyes when they look upon his own person." Alexander Pope

Take some time to reflect upon these questions:
- How do you view yourself?
- Do you see a beautiful person when you look in the mirror?

Chapter 8: Love the Skin You Are In

- Do you perceive yourself to be wise, compassionate, loving, and joyful?
- How do you converse with yourself?
- What words do you use to describe yourself out loud and silently?
- Are you kind and forgiving with yourself?
- How do you engage with yourself?
- Do you do special things for yourself?
- Do you engage in positive or negative self-talk?
- Do you hold grudges against yourself or let it go and keep it moving?

I've been on a journey of self-love for a while and can say in this moment that I have been influenced by many but defined by none. The journey wasn't easy, and in fact it is not over. Self-love, like self-reflection, is an ongoing ritual; it must be given intentional energy every day. I've arrived at a place of knowing *for sure* who I am and why I exist, and loving every part of who I am: the good, the bad, and the ugly, as they say. We are imperfect beings and will always be in a state of transformation—absorbing, learning, and growing in each moment of our lives.

Self-love for me is about being deeply authentic and transparent. I put little stock in what people think of me; I do what I want to do instead of allowing others to define my steps. I say how I feel (with as much honesty and compassion as I can) and go to bed every night knowing that I have lived by my core values and have not compromised my integrity. This to me is authentic living.

Self-love is also about accepting that you are who you are and working to become a better person each day. It's about knowing that you have limitations and intentionally working to turn them into strengths. Self-love is a journey, not a destination, because you will always have moments of uncertainty—moments when you will have to take a good look in the mirror or have a deep conversation with yourself. However, I do believe there is a place of arrival when self-love becomes easier, more natural, and automatic… a place and time when there is less struggle and more ease and grace.

When you finally arrive at *this place* you honor yourself, you speak your truth, you celebrate your inner core, you create and live with joy, you forgive yourself, you open your heart, you unselfishly share your love, and ultimately you love your life.

Self-love allows you to be authentically you. Being authentic is about loving the skin you are in, despite your faults. It is about speaking your mind in a way that truly expresses your values. Being authentic is about creating a consistent balance between how you think and feel and the way in which you live your life.

While I realize you (like many other women) may have been hurt, damaged, and maybe even abused at some point in your life, mistreatment is not the be-all and end-all of your life. I'm sure you've heard many stories of women who've experienced very hurtful or traumatic events yet found the courage to heal from within and overcome feelings of pain and self-doubt. Oprah Winfrey, an inspirational icon now, once was filled with pain and misery as a result of abuse. But look at her now! She knew that her painful experiences were not the end of her life but the beginning of a life of greatness. Sometimes the events we experience, painful or otherwise, prepare us for the divine purpose in our lives. And as you can see, although Oprah has everything she needs, wants, and desires, she is still on the journey of self-love. I believe she will finally arrive at "that place" where she will be comfortable in her own skin. You, too, will arrive at this place as long as you are very clear about what "this place" looks like for you. Be influenced by many but be defined by none! Create the life of your dreams on your terms and by your definitions only!

Delicious Living Tip #8
A savvy woman knows the value of protecting, preserving, and restoring her emotional and mental energy. Give your energy ONLY to things you are passionate about and to people who appreciate and respect you, your time, and your energy...

Food for Thought

What ingredients did you extract from this chapter to create your own recipe for a delicious life? Use the space below to record your thoughts.

Delicious!

Chapter 9
Release Your Juicy Joy

Joy is knowing for sure that you were uniquely designed to live with ease, grace, and abundance, and there are no limits on your life...

Joy: delight, pleasure, enjoyment, elation, bliss, euphoria.

A savvy woman living a delicious life is a joyous woman. Let me make this more clear. She "is" a *joyous* woman—not a happy woman, a joyous woman. Happiness is a moment in time, while joy is enduring and everlasting. Happiness is situational, meaning that one day you can be happy and the next not so happy. When you are joyous, joy is with you all the time.

Joy is sought by people all around the world. Even in third world countries where life is more difficult than we could imagine, people seek joy and often find it in the simplicity of life. People relentlessly search for joy as if it were a needle in a haystack hidden so deep as to never be found. Many people get so caught up in themselves and consumed with how life is so unfair to them that they lose sight of the fact that joy is in them all time.

Are you seeking more joy in your life? Have you reached the point of apathy and complacency? If joy knocked on your door and said hello, would you recognize its voice?

I have heard many definitions of joy. Merriam-Webster's online dictionary defines joy as "the emotion evoked by well-being, success or good fortune or by the prospect of possessing what one desires." Does this definition clarify the meaning of joy for you? Let's look at another definition, this one from Wikipedia. They define joy as happiness. That definition doesn't work, because it leaves you to define what happiness means. Here's a better one: dictionary.com defines joy as "an emotion of great delight or happiness caused by something exceptionally good or satisfying." Although it's still unclear, it gives a little more insight into the meaning of joy. The reality is that joy means many things to many people, thus supporting the notion that joy is within you and defined by you only. So how do *you* define joy?

What does joy mean to you? (Write your definition here.)

Defining joy on your own terms is essential to creating and living a delicious life. The ability to fully experience joy is a gift; to experience it deeply and consistently is a divine gift. I believe that we have the power to create joy, and it begins with mindful intention. Life is not waiting to be discovered—it is happening right now, in this present moment. Joy is the same. You have the innate power to either create or resist joy. You create joy by first believing that joy exists and that you deserve to experience it. In order to experience more joy, you must slow down and step away from your normal routine of life. It will serve you well to take time and reflect upon things and people

Delicious!

that bring you joy, then find ways to incorporate them into your life more often.

The best way to experience more joy is to move away from routines, schedules, and "to do" lists. Each of these is a form of obligation, thus creating the burden of having to do something. Joy is a state of being, not an act. When you live your life based on timelines and schedules, you are in a state of doing. When your life is anchored in living on energy, it frees you from the daily burdens of lists, schedules, and "to do" lists. I encourage you to focus your mental, spiritual, physical, and emotional energy on how you want to BE in each moment. *Being* allows you to fully experience the moments of life. When you are "being" in life, you can feel when joy is present or absent. The following steps may help you to release your juicy joy!

Tips for releasing your joy 79

1. Slow down and determine whether joy is present or absent in your spirit.
2. Define what joy means and feels like to you.
3. Make a list of all the things that bring you joy, and do them often.
4. Live each day "being" instead of "doing." Give your time and energy to the things that release joy.
5. Get rid of the schedules, timelines, and "to do" lists and instead create rituals for your life.
6. Be mindful and fully awake in each moment.
7. Set the intention that you are consumed with joy, and take daily steps to create and experience joyful moments.
8. Remember that joy is now and that you have the power to create joy every day.

---

9. Make it part of your ritual to help others experience joy in their lives.
10. Embrace and celebrate each moment of your life with love and acceptance.

You'll know you have mastered the art of living joyfully when your life has more moments of pleasure, bliss, and delightful experiences. You will smile and laugh more, love deeper and stronger, and every day will be a day of new beginnings filled with intention to experience joy. Graciously show gratitude for what you have, and watch more joy ooze from your soul. Remember you are joy, you can create and experience joy, and you have the power to help others release their juicy joy!

> **Delicious Living Tip #9**
> *A savvy woman is joyful and shows gratitude for all that she has and is. If you show gratitude, the universe will bless you more abundantly, and if you live on purpose your provisions will be met...*

Food for Thought

What ingredients did you extract from this chapter to create your own recipe for a delicious life? Use the space below to record your thoughts.

Delicious!

Chapter 10
Speak Your Delicious Truth

Boldness is when you live by your core values, speak your truth, and use your values to fearlessly navigate through life…

Bold: brave, confident, forthright, audacious, risky, daring!

When you create a life you love and live it deliciously, you know and speak your authentic voice. What is an authentic voice? It is the voice that resonates from deep within your soul. An authentic voice is honest, fearless, compassionate, and wise. Your authentic voice is waiting to speak!

If you are not sure what your authentic voice is, take some time to fill in each of the blanks below with a word or phrase that honestly comes quickly for you. Don't overthink it. After filling in the blanks, see if there is a common theme of what's important to you—a theme that expresses what matters most in your life.

I am passionate about _____

_____

I feel compassion toward_____

_____

For me, the greatest tragedy would be_____

_____

I would really love to_____

_____

I am enthused when_____

_____

The most meaningful thing is _____

_____

I am inspired by_____

_____

I come alive when _____

_____

I like to think about_____

_____

I wonder why_____

_____

If I could change one thing in the world, it would be_____

_____

The most important thing in my life is_____

_____

Upon completing the statements above, do you see a theme in what you are passionate about? Do you see a purpose for your life? Do you see what your authentic voice is revealing about you, or do you recognize the intuitive voice waiting to speak?

Delicious!

What is the theme in the above statements?

What is the purpose for your life?

What are you passionate about?

How to begin speaking in your authentic voice
(How to speak your truth)

Imagine a world where women can speak from the heart. Imagine if you could always say what you feel, without fear, worry, or apprehension. Imagine that you could speak your inner voice at work, at home, and in the world. Many women fear speaking in their authentic voice because they don't want to appear domineering, masculine, "bitchy," or uncaring. Maybe you can remember walking away from a situation thinking, "I wish I had spoken up" or "Why didn't I say something?" If you cannot imagine a time or place where you could always speak from the heart, here are some thoughts to consider. Answer each of the following questions as honestly as you can.

Chapter 10: Speak Your Delicious Truth

When is it difficult to speak your truth?

Who is it difficult to speak your truth to?

Why is it difficult to speak your truth to them?

84

If you could let out something that has been buried inside and share it with the world, what would you say?

When you fail to speak your truth when you know you should have, how does that make your spirit feel?

Delicious!

What kind of conversations do you have with yourself that you do not share with the world?

If you could wake up tomorrow and BE who you desire to be without any worry, concern, or fear, who would you BE?

85

Tips on speaking the truth:
1. Know your own truth first: Who am I? Why do I exist? What is my purpose in life?
2. Speak from your compassionate voice: the voice that seeks to understand, embrace, and support.
3. Use "I" statements to describe how you feel, without demeaning or blaming the other person.
4. Be courageous and take risks to tell people how you really feel. Do it with clarity, intention, and consideration.
5. Continue conversing with your spirit to reveal your authentic voice (the real you, without any masks).

A savvy woman living a delicious life is authentic...

Deliciously authentic people seem to have the "wow" factor. This "wow" comes from the ease and consistency with which they bring their inner jewels to the surface. The "wow" comes from the fact they are joyfully satisfied with what is on the inside and therefore project that inner confidence to the outside world. Here are the qualities of people who are congruent, authentic, and filled with "wow":

- awareness of the moods and feelings of others
- awareness of their own feelings
- acceptance of self
- ability to live in the present moment
- enjoyment of people and a desire to bring out the best in them
- ability to build rapport with people
- ability to motivate and inspire
- understanding that listening is more important than talking
- emotional maturity
- well-tuned social radar and the ability to respond accordingly
- sense of purpose
- ability to see the big picture
- willingness to speak candidly about their feelings
- empathy and concern for others
- ability to respect and embrace differences
- ability to sense the feelings of others
- capacity to read the behavioral cues of others
- guidance from inner values
- awareness of how they come across to others
- ability to "work the room"

Delicious!

Authenticity allows you to have presence and charisma!

An authentic spirit evolves when you are able to be congruent—that is, when your inner being matches what you portray to the world.

Congruency (described in Chapter 11) allows you to be the same person no matter who you are with and no matter where you are. Congruence (unity within one's self) is living in balance.

Strategies for becoming congruent and authentic:

1. Make a list of your top five strengths.

2. Write a short paragraph describing how you think you show up in the world—on other words, how you think people perceive you in personal and professional relationships.

3. Ask people who know you well to tell you what they think your top five strengths are.

4. Compare your strengths list with the comments others have given you about your strengths, and see if others perceive your potential and contributions as you do.

5. Compare your perspective with that of others to see if who you present to the world is similar to the person you believe yourself to be. If there is a big difference, it may indicate that who you think you are may not be the "you" who is showing up in the world.

6. What you think, feel, and believe on the inside should consistently match what you show to the world. So answer this question: "When you are alone, stripped of all your money, assets, titles, and other outward characteristics, who are you really?" You must clearly define who the person is underneath all that stuff. That is your authentic self.

Characteristics of Authenticity
(partial list from *Soul Eruption*)

Authentic	*Inauthentic*
Defines self by own values	Looks to others for definition
Pleases self first	Pleases others first
Open and honest	Afraid to express self
Feels empowered	Feels helpless
Lives the way they think	Lives according to what others think
Confident in self and ability	Unsure about self and ability
Seeks to be their best	Concerned with impressing others
Takes responsibility	Blames others for mistakes
Expects a good life	Takes what they can get
Sees the good in people	Finds fault with people
Genuine approach	Superficial interactions with others
Stands up for self	Often feels like a victim

Delicious!

Discovering your authentic self and voice

Fill in each blank with words that best describe your true desire or feeling.

I love_____

_____

I am passionate about_____

_____

I feel compassion toward_____

_____

The greatest tragedy would be_____

_____

I would really love to_____

_____

I am enthused when_____

_____

The most meaningful thing is _____

_____

I am inspired by_____

_____

I come alive when _____

_____

I like to think about_____

_____

I wonder why_____

_____

If I could change one thing in the world, it would be ____

_____

The most important thing in my life is_____

_____

I value this most: _____

_____

My deepest wish is_____

_____

My biggest fear is _____

_____

I am most capable of _____

_____

I have a special ability to _____

_____

My greatest talent is _____

_____

I would do this for free_____

_____

I admire _____

_____

I need this to feel complete_____

_____

My dream job or career is _____

_____

This gives me satisfaction_____

_____

Delicious!

I need this to feel happy_____

_____

This person would be a great mentor_____

_____

I am willing to take a risk on _____

_____

The vision for my life is _____

_____

My top three priorities are _____

_____

People say I am good at_____

_____

People describe me as _____

_____

I feel compelled to _____

_____

It is right to _____

_____

I feel connected to _____

_____

I am creative when _____

_____

My heart feels for _____

_____

Food for Thought

What ingredients did you extract from this chapter to
create your own recipe for a delicious life? Use the space
below to record your thoughts.

Delicious!

Chapter 11
Tell the Little Princess to Take a Hike

Congruency is when you treat yourself as fantastically as you treat others... and when you smile at the world with the same honesty and intensity with which you smile within...

Congruency: harmony, consistency, balance, ease, and grace!

There is a little princess in all of us, and there is a full-grown woman as well. The little princess is our "girl" self who sometimes overshadows the full-grown woman and can become our own demise. When these two parts of us are out of line, we ultimately are living incongruently or out of balance.

Let's talk about the little girl or princess who lives within us as women. She is often immature, self-centered, envious, catty, controlling, whiny, and insecure. Think back to your younger adolescent days of middle and high school. Can you recall the cliques and how girls betrayed, preyed upon, and ostracized other girls? I too once was involved in those types of shenanigans and recall the pain and misery I felt and caused on occasion. Those were moments of transformation as we tried to figure out who we were and where we stood in the world of other people and especially other females. I remember judging other girls by how they looked, what they did, and who they hung out with, and knowing that I too was under that same social microscope. Although I was generally pretty authentic and a leader versus a follower, I too fell victim to and perpetrator of the "mean girl" syndrome. Through my personal transformation I realized there is no place for the little princess or the mean girl syndrome in my life. Yet, as you may have discovered, there are plenty of grown (in age) women who still allow this way of living and engaging to permeate their lives.

Is the little princess reigning in your life?

Let me back up and explain what I mean by *girl* versus *woman*. Think back to your middle school and high school days. You can probably recall incidents when you or other girls participated in the "mean girl" games. You know what I am talking about: the gossiping, snickering, leaving certain girls out, judging and classifying other girls, cliques against cliques, and so on. I believe we all know and have either been the victim or perpetrator in these types of games. Now, think about how the victims must have felt and how nasty and emotionally draining this type of behavior was. Those were girl behaviors. At this point in your life, ideally you have graduated from the school of girlhood and emerged as a full-grown, whole woman.

Unlike a girl, a woman is confident in her own skin. She's satisfied with who she is, no matter what titles and credentials she does or does not hold. She doesn't take everything personally, knows her core values and lives by them, and treats others with kindness and respect. What another woman wears, what she looks like, and whether she is pretty or not does NOT matter to a woman, because a woman sees the souls of other women not their outward definitions. I could continue, but you get the picture. A woman does not play those schoolgirl games.

These "mean girl" games continue to show up in our lives and careers today. If you've recently said or thought "Who does she think she is?" you may still have traces of "girl" flowing through your veins. The little princess (girl) inside wants all the attention, gets emotional when things don't go her way, pouts and maybe even cries at the drop of a hat, thinks the world should revolve around her etc. The little princess wants the best Barbie, has to be the mommy or teacher when playing games, gets jealous when her friends play with other friends—and the scenarios continue.

Okay, now for the point of all this: Who wants to be around someone like the little princess? Who wants to hire or promote her? Who wants to date her? Who wants to be on her team? I may be going out on a limb here, but I would say "No one!"

The little princess in you still functions from a place of insecurity and false feelings of superiority. On rare occasions she shows up in my life; however, I have intentionally told her to go take a hike and get out of my way so the whole, full-grown, mature woman in me can reign. Yes, in my queendom there is absolutely no room for the little princess—only the queen diva (**D**ivine, **I**nspirational, **V**ibrant, **A**spiring) sister in me rules my space.

What I know to be true is that the little princess causes many women to live an incongruent life. The little princess is alive and kicking on the inside, yet often women will try

Chapter 11: Tell the Little Princess to Take a Hike

to portray something else to the world. A full-grown woman—a savvy woman—lives in balance and has declared dominion over her queendom with no tolerance for the little princess' existence.

You may be wondering by now if your little princess shows up in your life more than you want her to or whether you would be classified as a full-grown, whole woman. The following are characteristics of women (people) who are living congruently, in balance and harmony. See how many of these characteristics apply to you, describing how you live your life and how you show up in the world.

You are living congruently when...
- Your outer self mirrors your inner self and vice versa.
- The person you display to the world is the same person you are in private.
- You give yourself as much as you give others.
- You do what you say you will do.
- You display internal and external consistency throughout all aspects of life.
- You are perceived as sincere by others.
- You can be authentically yourself, despite the situation or the company you keep.
- You are transparent...people see the real you.
- Others have described you by saying, "What you see is what you get."

Unity within one's self is essential to living a delicious life. We all have moments when we put on a mask to impress others or be accepted. I encourage you to take off the many masks and let your juicy goodness (authentic

Delicious!

reflection) speak for itself. When you achieve congruence, you will have the courage to live your life according to your inner needs and desires, rather than the demands of society.

How to become congruent:
- Make a list of the behaviors you show the world and the ones you display in private, and then compare them to see if there is consistency.
- Discover the real you and let your true essence be apparent to world.
- Stop trying to please everyone else, and please yourself first.
- Say what you mean, and mean what you say.
- Speak from the heart and communicate directly.
- When someone has offended you, tell them instead of complaining to others or holding it in.
- Be mindful of how you come across to others.
- Be genuine in your words and actions.
- Don't try to fit in; just be yourself.
- Always act from a place of integrity.

The more congruent you are, the greater will be the amount of vibrancy, peace, and satisfaction you experience. When you are congruent, you are true to yourself, and when you are true to yourself you can be true to others and in every aspect of your life.

Affirmations for living a congruent life:
- ❖ I will not let others define my success.
- ❖ I know what's good for me, and I will bring goodness into my life.

Chapter 11: Tell the Little Princess to Take a Hike

- ❖ I am the architect of my life.

- ❖ I deserve to have what the world has to offer.

- ❖ I will listen to that little voice that says "you can do it" even when I am afraid.

- ❖ I will stop looking outward and begin looking inward and upward.

- ❖ It's not where I live that is important, but how I live is critical.

- ❖ I cannot control anyone or anything else, but I am in charge of my own thoughts and behavior.

Using these affirmations and practicing daily intentional behaviors anchored in self-love and wholeness will allow you to keep the little princess at bay. If she is boldly present in your life at this moment, please tell her to get out of the way so the full-grown, whole woman inside you can emerge...

Delicious!

Delicious Living Tip #11

A savvy woman is a whole woman: a woman who is committed to letting go of the little princess within. Be sure to intentionally absorb positive, fulfilling sources of energy each day and do a toxic release before you go to bed (read, pray, meditate, exercise, etc.).

Chapter 11: Tell the Little Princess to Take a Hike

Food for Thought

What ingredients did you extract from this chapter to create your own recipe for a delicious life? Use the space below to record your thoughts.

Delicious!

Chapter 12
Preserve Your Deliciousness

Preservation is when you mindfully and diligently work to restore and sustain your emotional, mental, and spiritual energy source...

Preserve: protect, conserve, save, defend, sustain, care for.

Your deliciousness is all the goodness you have inside. It's the way you think, the way you love, and how you share your emotions. Deliciousness is the private juice within your soul.

Your deliciousness is often only given to or shared with those you really care about—the people who really matter in your life. Your deliciousness lives in your sacred circle, the place where you keep your secrets, dreams, desires, and aspirations. Within your deliciousness is the BEST you: the loving, caring, wise, compassionate, ambitious, vibrant you. Your deliciousness is like honey in a beehive, the pearl in a sea shell... it is the essence of why you exist, and the treasure within that makes you unique and sweet. In your deliciousness is where your passion and purpose lives. It is the intimate place where all your juicy goodness is stored, and I like to call this deliciousness your emotional and spiritual energy.

A savvy woman does not allow toxic people to invade her sacred circle. She has mastered the art of intuition and knows how to determine who is for her and who is against her. A delicious life is one where your emotional energy is full, alive, and well protected. If you desire to live a delicious life, you may need to get rid of the toxic people in your life.

Do you have toxic people in your life? Are some of these people family members or close friends? Are they consuming your precious emotional energy, draining away your deliciousness, and sucking the life out of you? If you answered yes to these questions, then you will have to do something to maintain your emotional energy.

Emotional energy is your life source. It is the heartbeat of your soul and your guide for living. It is also the driving force behind your ability to exist in the world. If your emotional energy supply is inadequate you may find yourself barely getting through life and often running on fumes!

Delicious women preserve their emotional energy so they can radiate a flavorful aroma. Think of your emotional energy (deliciousness) as a battery. A fully charged battery makes things happen and gets things done. Remember that your deliciousness is your source of love, wisdom, compassion, ambition, and vibrancy. When a battery is weak or low, things slow down and even shut down completely. For example, let's say you are ready to take pictures at an important event such as a graduation or a wedding and all of a sudden the low battery light comes on in your camera. Next thing you know, you've missed your opportunity to capture one of the most important moments of a lifetime. Unless you have a charger or spare batteries on hand, you can never recapture this moment. Doesn't that feeling just make you sick? Well, that's what happens when your emotional energy is low. All of a sudden you just give up, stop striving, stop working, and you miss out on the beautiful moments in life.

You must relentlessly protect and nurture your deliciousness. It is the essence of who you are; it is your lifeline and the pulse of your life. It's up to you to make sure you have a charger, spare batteries, and that your battery does not become weak. When all is said and done, your deliciousness is your juicy goodness! Every time you allow someone to steal drops of your goodness, you allow your cup to become empty. A delicious woman's cup should be overflowing with goodness, not only for herself but also so she will have enough to fill the cups of the people who really matter to her. Please don't allow people, places, events, and tasks to steal your goodness, because you need it to live a delicious life.

Here are some tips for preserving and replenishing your deliciousness:

1. *Identify your battery charger (your source of positive and replenishing energy).* Discover and use your higher power. That could be church, God, Buddha, or whatever you believe in. Set aside time each day to pray or meditate so you can rebuild your inner strength and replenish your spiritual energy.
2. *Don't allow your batteries to run down (set and maintain emotional boundaries).* Identify the people who are sucking you dry and either remove them from your life or only allow yourself to engage with them on a limited or superficial basis. When they come around, envision an invisible barrier that protects you from their nagging, complaining, or miserable personality.

3. *Keep your spare batteries close at hand (people, places, or activities that provide support and encouragement).* Make sure you have at least three people in your life who are positive and encouraging—people who believe in you and do not have negative attitudes—and seek them out when you need a pep talk. Be careful not to steal their energy by nagging and complaining; go to them for solutions rather than focusing on problems. Finally, discover and utilize the activities that bring you peace and joy. If you enjoy swimming, cooking, or exercising, do this activity as often as you can.

To protect and preserve your emotional energy, it is important that you release the negative toxins that you take in from life and that you realize that you deserve to be toxin-free. Start paying attention to how you feel deep inside when certain people are in your presence. Turn your people radar on full blast. If someone makes you feel exhausted or stressed out, they may be toxic. If someone makes you say inside, "Oh no, here they come," they may be toxic. On the other hand, if someone makes you feel strong and empowered, figure out how you can be around that person more. If someone makes you feel energized and joyful, learn what is special about that person so you can get some of that wonderful positive energy for yourself.

Life is a choice! How you live it is a greater choice! Choose to live deliciously and toxin-free. Learn how to protect your emotional energy and preserve your juicy goodness. Most of all, learn how to be a battery charger for others!

Delicious!

Food for Thought

What ingredients did you extract from this chapter to create your own recipe for a delicious life? Use the space below to record your thoughts.

Delicious!

Chapter 13
A Savvy Woman Always Takes the High Road

Control is when you are fully in
the driver's seat of your life,
doing what you want to do, living
how you want to live, and being
who you want to be…

Control: influence, direct, manage, choose!

A savvy woman is wise, intuitive, discerning, and
strategic. She is fully awakened to what is going on in her
life, and she can sport a detour or a distraction in her
journey a mile away.

A savvy woman doesn't fight every battle that presents
itself. Instead, she knows the power in saving her
deliciousness for all things purpose-filled and destiny-
driven. You do not have time for naysayers, naggers,
complainers, and dream stealers.

A deliciously savvy woman saves her energy for the
war! That's right—she is prepared for the big battles that
may arise in life, the moments when it really matters.
These are the moments when she has to fight for what she
believes in, including her dreams, her vision, and her
livelihood.

You may be on the battlefield and not even know it. Are you on the battlefield? Are you literally or mentally fighting with others? Are you trying to prove yourself to someone? Are you trying to win someone over with no luck? If you answered yes to any of these questions, you are on the battlefield. That's okay, because you will soon learn how to stop fighting the battles and claim victory in the war. This is your time—the moment when you learn how to become attuned to your emotions and thoughts and use them to navigate your way to the high road. You must become a master at hearing and responding accurately to the voice of intuition, the voice that leads, guides, and directs your footsteps toward your higher purpose in life. A savvy woman always chooses to take the high road in life. Do not waste your time on people who are traveling the low roads. View them as a distraction alongside the road to your destiny.

Realize that you can't win every battle, nor should you seek to do so . . .

Why fight battles and be worn down when it's time to go to war? These small battles in your life are distractions in your journey to your greatness, your divine destiny! Choose the people or issues that deserve your precious energy. It is critical that you save your deliciousness for fulfilling your divine destiny. Fight only the battles that will elevate you spiritually and emotionally. You don't need the approval of those who pretend they don't see you or those who minimize your greatness. Let go of these people, stop fighting those battles, and watch what happens. The people you need will come. The people who are genuine

Delicious!

will come. The people who will support, accept, and celebrate you will come.

Don't let toxic people drain you dry. If you do, you will be too exhausted to energize your purpose and embrace the divine opportunities that come your way. The secret to failure is trying to please everybody. The secret to winning is choosing your battles and saving your energy for the war.

You may be wondering why I use the words "war" and "battle" in my depiction of life. I do so because sometimes life can present issues and circumstances that make you feel as though you are in combat. .Life can feel like you are fighting with others and often fighting against yourself. Many people fight to stay alive, they fight to be successful, and they fight to just make it through the day. This is an unfortunate place to be, but it is not YOUR destiny!

I don't know about you, but the God I serve is a loving God...a God who wants us to have the best and be the best. As my grandmother said, "God is delicious," and he wants you to be delicious too! As you co-create your delicious life, know that it is your God-given right to live the most satisfying and rewarding life that you can imagine. So discover, release, replenish, and preserve your deliciousness for all the things that are coming your way.

I give you permission to restore your self-love. I give you permission to celebrate your goodness. I give you permission to simply *just be you*. Don't worry about what other people think of you; don't worry about what they might say. Do your thing, produce and seek to please yourself. When you do this, those who ignored you will have no choice but to see your greatness! And if they are lucky, you might just let them get a taste of it! A delicious woman knows how to show up, show out, and be victorious in her life.

A few suggestions on choosing your battles and claiming victory:
1. When you feel like someone is luring you into battle, ask yourself, "Will engaging in this battle take me to my highest level?"
2. When you feel like you are being sucked in, stop and determine whether winning the battle will move you one step closer to your divine purpose or goals in life.
3. If you keep trying to impress someone and they continue to ignore you, move on to the next great thing. They are not worth your time. (They really see you and in fact see your greatness and just may feel intimidated by it).
4. If you are trying to connect with someone and they don't return your calls or respond to your emails, or if they ignore you when they see you; just accept the fact that your relationship with them was not meant to be. Give your energy to those who are genuinely interested in you.
5. The next time you feel frustrated, ignored, or unappreciated, recognize that these feelings are a distraction that could take you off your path. Resist the temptation to engage.

Every day, every second, you have the power to choose what you will fight for. Choose to fight for the things that bring you peace, comfort, stability, and movement. Don't let others wear you down before the real battles begin. The real battles are the obstacles you must overcome to deliciously walk out your destiny.

When you are overflowing with juicy goodness and focused on reaching your goals, everything and everyone you need to be victorious

Delicious!

*will appear when you least expect it. Walk it out, girlfriend, and be
sure to take bold, sassy steps in your delicious stilettos!*

Delicious Living Tip #13

*A savvy woman wins the war because she preserves
her emotional energy instead of fighting every battle.
A delicious woman knows better than to waste her
juicy goodness on things that do not matter.*

Chapter 13: A Savvy Woman Always Takes the High Road

Food for Thought

What ingredients did you extract from this chapter to create your own recipe for a delicious life? Use the space below to record your thoughts.

Delicious!

Chapter 14
Show Up and Show Out

Presence is the ability to share space with others and profoundly penetrate the room with a powerful aura that attracts people…

Presence: charisma, aura, authority, poise, allure, magnetism!

A savvy woman is a woman of presence, and a delicious life affords you many opportunities to show up and show out. What do I mean? When you show up, you step into any situation and are confidently and boldly present. When you show out, you captivate those around you, make a powerful impression, and leave them wanting more. A savvy woman living a delicious life has mastered the art of presence. She knows how to show up and show out.

Becoming a woman of presence can be a reality that no longer has to be dreamt about. How would people describe your personality, style, and ability to engage with others? Have you heard words used such as *amazing, stunning, magical, splendid,* or *engaging?* When you walk into a room, do you get the sense that people are silently saying, "Wow, who's that?" or when you speak in any forum or situation do you see the physical expressions of others saying, "Yes, tell me more"? Those things happen to people who have presence.

Here is another example. Remember how Ms. Celie followed Shug Avery (in the movie *The Color Purple*) around everywhere and said she was like honey? (Go ahead, laugh out loud.) Well, Shug Avery had presence. Ms. Shug was delicious! Despite the undercurrents of her character, Ms. Shug knew how to capture the attention of men and women.

Becoming a woman of presence begins with belief in oneself. If you don't believe that you are capable, dynamic, stunning, or magical, how is anyone else going to believe it? Ms. Shug was a delicious woman...

Who do you hold in high esteem? Is there one woman who has it going on, one woman you secretly admire for her poise, boldness, charisma, and presence? Determine who that is, write down every characteristic she possesses, and define what that looks like for you. We are unique beings, and therefore you must develop our own unique style of presence. If you are daring and willing to take the risk, make contact with this dynamic woman. Tell her she is dynamic and that you admire her presence. Then take it a step further and ask, "How did you develop the art of presence?" Yes, this requires you to think and believe that there are other women out there who are just as delicious as you! Just think what could happen if we all really believed this and acted upon it.

Let's talk a little more about presence. Presence is the ability to share space with others and profoundly penetrate the room with a powerful aura that attracts people. Let's face it, you want to be seen, heard, valued, appreciated, and respected. If you live your life like a wallflower, that is unlikely to happen. No one hears the silent voice in the back of the room. No one respects a woman who does not respect herself. No one pays attention to a woman who doesn't pay attention to how she is showing up in the world. Lastly, no one appreciates a woman who does not appreciate herself and allows others to walk all over her. You may be too shy, modest, or humble to admit it, but I know that somewhere inside, you secretly desire to be a woman of presence. Why? Because a woman of presence is not a perfect woman but a beautiful masterpiece of imperfection who loves every flaw and awkward piece of herself. A woman of presence is a woman who charismatically gets what she wants, goes where she wants, has what she wants to have, and lives life out loud.

Being a woman of presence is not about being conceited, flamboyant, and arrogant but rather about being comfortable in your own skin despite your flaws and idiosyncrasies. So don't be afraid to be a woman of presence; it is a beautiful thing to stand in your own space with confidence.

It is your duty and responsibility to become of woman of presence. There are young women looking to you for guidance and direction. It is our duty as women to create and leave a legacy for our young sisters to emulate and pass on to their younger sisters. Think about it—where would you or I be without the dynamic women who came before us and the dynamic women of our time? I am proud to say that women like Oprah Winfrey, Michelle Obama, Queen Latifah, Jada Pinkett Smith, Tyra Banks, and other fabulous women have helped shaped the woman I have become. But the amazing thing is that I believe when given the opportunity to meet these delicious diamonds in person that I will shine just as bright in my own sweet and savvy way. There is NO woman better than you; however, there are women who shine differently from you. A delicious woman of presence believes this, knows this, and lives her life accordingly.

All too often, women are afraid to give props to another woman—to tell another woman she is fabulous—yet we want other women to do that for us. Let's keep it real. There are millions of women in the world, and many of them are delicious. The key is not to strive to become a carbon copy of another woman but to put your unique ingredients together to create the most deliciously fabulous YOU! You've heard it before: "Only a diamond can cut another diamond." That means you must be comfortable enough in your own skin to share space with other diamonds…other delicious women.

If you want to begin living a delicious life or make your life more scrumptious, then identify other delicious women and learn from them. Manifesting the life you desire takes a vision, belief, and daily intentional actions. So, think about the "best" life you could live. Imagine what the "best" you looks like, and create a plan to create your "best life" reality.

Tips on creating your delicious life recipe…
1. Define what your best life looks like specifically. Write it down with a timeline and plan. Set specific dates and goals.
3. Sit quietly and imagine yourself living your best life. What are you doing, where do you live, who is in your life, how much money are you earning, how are you specifically making a contribution to humanity?
4. Envision yourself doing what you dream of. Where are you? What are people saying? How do you feel?
5. Hold that image and those feelings in your head. Really feel the feelings and imagine "it" coming into your being… now let it go!

Delicious!

6. Write down the things you need to do to make it happen. Make a list of the people you need to connect with. Repeat steps one through five several times a day until you know for sure what your best you, your best life, looks like.

Show up and show out!

Here are ten suggestions that will help you to be radiantly vibrant every day and *show up and show out:*

1. Always know and remember that there is no one like you in the world. You are uniquely created to live out your divine purpose on your own terms.
2. Discover your inner jewels (talents and skills), and share them with the world unselfishly.
3. Wake up and see the possibilities in life instead of the challenges.
4. Do something every day to create the life you want.
5. Take time out for yourself. Take care of yourself.
6. Seek to make someone else feel appreciated and special.
7. Speak your authentic voice—never compromise your personal values or integrity.
8. Change your thoughts to reflect what you want instead of what you *don't* want.
9. Pulsate with energy. Be awakened in each moment. Be alive in all you do. Do everything with passion and purpose.
10. Create intentions for your life and speak them daily, focusing your thoughts on what you desire.

Still unclear about what a delicious woman looks like and or sounds like? I offer you the Catriceology blueprint of the epitome of the delicious woman...

A Glimpse into a Delicious Woman
Soul ~~~Enduring
Spirit~~~ Unwavering
Mind~~~ Clever
Heart~~~ Charitable
Purpose~~~ Divine
Vision~~~ Vivid
Personality~~~ Magnetic
Attitude~~~ Optimistic
Word~~~ Sincere
Thoughts~~~ Strategic
Behavior~~~ Virtuous
Actions~~~ Intentional
Feelings~~~ Intense
Love~~~ Passionate
Intentions~~~ Pure
Approach~~~ Compassionate
Integrity~~~ Authentic
Voice~~~ Influential

Now it's your turn. Fill in each blank with one word describing each delicious part of you or your plan and recipe for how you want to show up in the world.

Soul _____

Spirit _____

Mind _____

Heart_____

Purpose _____

Delicious!

Vision_____

Personality_____

Attitude _____

Word_____

Thoughts _____

Behavior_____

Actions_____

Feelings_____

Love_____

Intentions_____

Approach_____

Integrity_____

Voice_____

Style _____

Appearance _____

Communication _____

Image_____

Future _____

Delicious Living Tip #14

A savvy woman knows the power of her internal radiance. Remember that it is your light and your shine that matter most. Find ways to shine your light in the world and help others discover their light. Remember that a delicious woman is one who carries herself boldly and with presence.

Food for Thought

What ingredients did you extract from this chapter to create your own recipe for a delicious life? Use the space below to record your thoughts.

Delicious!

Chapter 15
Magnetize and Release the Delicious Woman in You

Magnetizing is the ability to draw unto yourself the innermost desires of your heart with ease and grace…

Magnetize: charm, fascinate, attract, appeal.

Have you ever met someone who was so wonderfully captivating that your breath was taken away by their mere existence? I have met several people like this, and they left a lasting impression upon me. People like this don't often show up in your daily life, but if they do, you are very lucky! If you have not met someone like this, I guarantee you will know it when it happens.

People like this have a certain kind of magnetic "power," if you will—an energy vibration that sends a steady, pulsating stream of fascination and intrigue. Not all magnetic vibrations are so bold and overt. Some people leave a more subtle impression that is subliminal and lingering, the kind that sneaks up on you and makes you smile on the inside after leaving their presence. Regardless of whether their energy is subtle or vivacious, there's a common rhythm to their message. Magnetic people exude a genuine spirit, have a positive attitude, exhibit an inviting personality, vocalize powerful words, move with grace, display integrity, and smile with their eyes just to name a few traits they have in common.

Some say people are born with this magnetic quality, and while I partially agree I also believe anyone can become more magnetic. Magnetic people tend to get what they want out of life simply by captivating whomever they encounter.

What does being magnetic have to do with living a deliciously vibrant life? Every human thought and action is made up of energy and vibrations. We expend energy (emotional, physical, mental, and spiritual) in every single moment, and through that energy we send verbal and nonverbal messages about what's in our mind, heart, and soul. The more positive energy you send, the more you get back. The greater your positive impact on the lives of others, the richer your life will be. The more you give to others, the more you will receive in return. While many of us live to give, let's keep it real: we want to receive as well. It could be as simple as receiving a raise, a promotion, an invitation, or special recognition. If you want certain things to manifest within your life, you have to give freely and learn how to attract what you want by broadcasting a message that says, "Here I am, I ain't going anywhere, and I deserve all the good things available to me."

Take a look at your life as it is right now. If it is not what you desire, maybe you are not giving enough intentional mental energy to the things you desire. Again, what you think about grows in your life. Remember that the things you *don't* want will grow, too, if that's where you're investing your mental energy. Choose your thoughts wisely, and harness your power to create a vibrantly delicious life!

Delicious!

Seven savory ways to release the delicious woman within:

1. Discover and write down the five most beautiful, unique, or fabulous things about you. Spend consistent, quality time polishing your strengths. Then flaunt them! Don't worry about what other people think; just *do* you and *be* you.

2. Discover the things that make you feel alive inside, make your heart sing, and bring you ridiculous joy. Doing these things will help you reveal your inner light and release your juicy goodness.

3. Discover the things about you that you think are ordinary, and then make them extraordinary. Food for thought: people eat with their eyes first. That means you may only have one moment, one opportunity to demonstrate your deliciousness when it really matters. Learn how to showcase your strengths and add shine to your limitations. Extraordinary people get the job, get the gig, get called back, get promoted... they just get more than those who are ordinary. Be extraordinarily delicious in every moment.

4. Discover your unique flavor and separate yourself from the crowd. Remember that a delicious woman is a woman who captivates others, commands attention, and takes people's breath away. You cannot experience this delicious power if you choose to be a wallflower in life. Create your delicious persona, one that is natural and authentic, not a mask or a façade. Create a social style and a personal brand that makes people think, "Wow! Who's that?" Let's face it; the power lies in who knows you and not what you know most of the time. If you want to create a "who knows

you" persona, you have to be a delicious woman of presence. You must be memorable if you want to be remembered, and your soul scent and your juicy goodness is what will leave the lingering aroma that stays with people after you've left the room.

5. Begin developing your Delicious Brand. Think of your favorite clothes designer or favorite restaurant, and determine why you love them. What makes them so special and appealing to you? Why do you keep going back for more of their product? Find out what it is that makes you want more of what they have to offer. They obviously offer something that is so good you want more. That is exactly the delicious brand you want to develop: a clear, profound, and unique flavor that only you can offer to the world... a flavor so good that people will seek you out, want more of your goodness (time, product, service, personality, etc.) and tell others about you.

6. Joyfully yet strategically sprinkle your juicy goodness in the world. When you pour your juicy goodness into those who matter, your cup will overflow with the things you desire. Focus on giving delicious service to others, for if you are not living to give, you are not living deliciously. A delectable cookie that never gets eaten is a waste of great ingredients, so share your goodness with others unselfishly.

Delicious Living Tip #15 *A savvy woman knows how to attract what she desires by being a person that others notice and remember. Walk with confidence, stand tall and strong, speak up and be heard… and most importantly, seek to create an impression that lingers long after you've left the room.*

Chapter 15: Magnetize and Release the Delicious Woman in You

Food for Thought

What ingredients did you extract from this chapter to create your own recipe for a delicious life? Use the space below to record your thoughts.

Delicious!

Chapter 16
Cash In on Your Delicious Charisma

Charisma is when you comfortably engage with others in a way that fascinates them into wanting to learn more and more about you...

Charismatic: captivating, mesmerizing, dynamic!

Charisma is that unspoken quality that mysteriously attracts other people to you. When you have charisma, it gives you the social confidence to remain true to yourself regardless of who you are interacting with or the social setting you are in.

A charismatic woman knows how to work the room, engage others, and ultimately get what she wants without necessarily manipulating them. Charisma affords you the freedom to just "be" who you are, without any masks. A charismatic woman has the uncanny ability to be charming, likeable, magnetic, and mesmerizing. If you've ever met someone and wondered why you were attracted to them like bees on honey, most likely they had a charismatic personality.

People with social confidence are able to share their most intimate selves and be transparent in their engagements—something many people secretly wish they could do. A socially confident woman is also intuitive, meaning she can sense, read, and interpret the feelings of others and respond in a way that makes them feel seen, heard, and validated. Another benefit of her intuition is that she can quickly sense whether people are for her or against her. This is an essential skill for living deliciously, especially when it comes to preserving your deliciousness. Remember the importance of preserving your deliciousness as it is your life source. Without adequate amounts of juicy goodness you emotionally die; you stop living and merely exist instead.

Social confidence (social known as social capital) is a valuable commodity. When you take away titles, money, and possessions, social capital is all we have left. Social capital is our word, our integrity, our personal image and how we show up in the world and engage with others. You

would be surprised how many people "make it" on social confidence/capital alone. So don't take this lightly—social confidence is invisible gold.

Before you learn more about cashing in on your delicious charisma, let's look at three primary traits of a socially confident woman and explore why social confidence is an essential aspect of a delicious woman.

Three primary traits of a socially confident woman:
- She loves the skin she is in and accepts herself as she is.
- She is aware of her presence and personal power and uses it to make others feel good and to attract what she desires.
- She lives in the moment and is fully awakened to life and those around her.

Delicious!

Part of living a deliciously vibrant life is being able to fully embrace your personal power and presence. Presence a form of charisma that allows you to occupy space and captivate people merely by being in the room, living in the moment, and loving the skin you are in. When you can just show up and make others feel good about themselves, you often magically get what you want. "How does this happen?" you might ask. People do business with people they like, people endorse people they like, people buy from people they like. When people like you, they are more likely to trust you and believe in you. When you are able to gain the belief and trust of others, you can then ask for what you want and need, and you will have a greater chance of getting a yes. Need I say more?

Using your social capital is how you cash in on your charisma! Remember when I said it was like invisible gold? Cha-ching! It's time to cash in on your deliciousness. Being a delicious woman is a beautiful, exciting, liberating way of living that has other benefits as well. One of my favorite quotations is from Charlie "Tremendous Jones," who said, "The only difference between where you are right now and where you will be next year at this same time are the people you meet and the books you read." The people you meet will surely either advance or obstruct your life success. The people you meet can either influence or sabotage your destiny. Therefore, it's important that you have the ability to do more than just meet people—you must be able to captivate people, take their breath away, and leave a lasting, luscious impression upon them. I guarantee that if you make lasting connections, doors will open and the desires of your heart will be granted. Of course, having connections will not do it alone, but they will be a nice chunk of the pie!

Here are seven things you can do to cash in on your charisma and create delicious relationships—connections that will fill you up and satisfy your personal and professional needs:

1. Be authentic and tell the truth. Don't try to be anyone other than who you are, and be transparent in your actions with others. Know your truth and speak your truth, because people do business with people they trust.

2. Focus on giving deeply and sincerely to the relationship, especially if you are "relating" with another delicious woman. A delicious woman will smell your shenanigans and foolish façade from a mile away. Give without expecting anything in return, do something to help them out, promote them, or connect them to another delicious person you know.

3. Be resourceful. Everybody is looking to gain something. Don't just take from the relationship; give back. Discover what they need or desire and find ways to help them achieve that. People love it when you help them, and they are more willing to help you.

4. Pay attention to what matters most to the other person. Be thoughtful and kind by remembering some of their favorites and surprising them with small tokens of appreciation. You know how good it feels to be appreciated, valued, and remembered.

5. Notice the things that often go unnoticed. Remember that a delicious woman is intuitive, aware, and awakened. Give sincere compliments, and offer words of encouragement. Comment on the things that are going on in their lives. An important element of charisma is making others feel good about themselves.

6. Netweave instead of networking. That means go to events for the pure enjoyment of it. Mingle and connect

Delicious!

with people without expectations, and save your elevator pitch or your 30-second commercial for the right moment. Focus on what you can do for others instead of what you want them to do for you. Turn your charisma up full strength and captivate others by your sincere concern and interest in what they do. Remember that people like people who make them feel good. By making others feel good, you will feel great and earn social capital points. That doesn't mean faking it and brown-nosing, it means making real human connections. (Do come prepared to deliver an irresistibly delicious elevator pitch, but be sure to intoxicate them with your soul scent first, so that by the time you give your 30-second commercial they will be mesmerized by every word you say.)

7. Realize and wholeheartedly believe in the power of living to give. As you can see, tips 1 through 6 were all about giving to get what you want. If you have mastered the art of being a delicious woman, then giving to others will not be a problem for you.

The most important actions you can take in building relationships are to show up, show out, and wow others without being arrogant or overbearing. A delicious woman captivates others with ease and grace, as if she was born to magnetize others. The key is to give what you want to receive, but be sure you are giving to the right people.

Delicious Living Tip #16

A savvy woman is not afraid to step boldly into the world and claim her space. You have only one life to live. Live each moment with confidence and intention. Be fully awakened to the power of your presence. A savvy woman knows how to cash in on her charisma!

Delicious!

Dessert Selections:
Tasty Life Tips and Tools
to Help You Create and Live
a Delicious Life

This book is only the beginning to living the life of your dreams. Stay tuned into Catriceology for more tasty tidbits and fabulous recipes for living the sweet life. I have shared a lot of information and offered numerous tips and strategies on

becoming a delicious woman. There is so much more to share, but I will save that for the next book. As I say in all of my workshops, take what works—in other words, eat the meat and spit out the bones. Use what works for you, and make it work for you.

At the beginning of this journey, I told you that you have everything you need to live a delicious life, and that still holds true. Your life is your own, and you have to discover and use your unique personal ingredients to create your best life. Take what I have given you and tweak it to fit you. Find your desired lifestyle, and whatever you do and however you choose to do it, make it irresistibly *delicious!*

Until we meet again, please do this for me and more importantly for yourself...

1. Unconditionally love the skin you are in, because it's phenomenally yours. Pamper yourself, love yourself, take special care of you and your juicy goodness, and celebrate you.

2. Discover your strengths and polish them up until they sparkle like gold! Release your juicy goodness and show up and show out.

3. Accept and embrace your flaws and limitations. Work on transforming your traits from ordinary to extraordinary.

4. Define your most delicious life on your own terms, live by your core values, and live life out loud. That means being fearless, mindful, awakened, intentional, and intuitive.

5. Dream big, have even bigger faith, and speak and breathe life into your dreams and the dreams of other women. Help expand the delicious movement.

6. Discover the things that make you feel alive inside: the things that make you tingle and fill you with joy. Take time to do them often. Give your deliciousness to the people and things that really matter.

7. Get out of your own way. Stop making excuses, procrastinating, and keeping your life on layaway. Take back your life and live it on your own terms. Step into your incredible personal power and boldly walk out the vision for your life.

8. Re-dedicate your life purpose to living to give. Give sincerely and unselfishly. Pour abundantly into the lives of the people who really matter. Savvy women understand the power of doing this.

Delicious!

9. Tell the little princess to take a hike. Kick her to the curb and tell her to get out of your way! A delicious woman does not have time for childish games. Always take the high road, because your stilettos are designed for high stepping.

10. Last but certainly not least, name it, claim it , believe it, and receive it. Whatever your "it" is, visualize it, magnetize it, attract it, breathe life into it, and receive it with open arms. In the meantime, put your sassy red stilettos on and walk it out. If you have to sprint, then get your sprint on and make a mad dash toward your delicious destiny! A sweet, sassy and satisfied destiny awaits you...

This is not the end of this book. You may have read this delicious little guide in its entirety, but there is much more to digest. In fact, this is a book you will surely read again and use often. As you can imagine, you will not become a delicious woman and or live a delicious life overnight. Becoming delicious from the inside out will take some time. So be sure to read this book many, many times. Use all of the exercises to help you create a delicious life you love. And in the spirit of living to give, you can't absolutely keep all this deliciousness to yourself, right? Of course not, so tell your girlfriends and family members about this book. Share it with them and or get them their own copy! My goal is to create a Delicious Woman movement; a new and scrumptious lifestyle epidemic. So will you help me spread the power of this sweet virus? Thanks in advance; I know you will share this book with all the women you know, and I appreciate you. I appreciate you for buying this book, reading this book, and using this book as your guide for living your most juicy and delicious life.

Thank you for taking the time to read this book. I hope you will use this guide to become delicious from the inside out! And until we meet again in the scrumptious world of Catriceology... just live your life and make sure it's undeniably, irresistibly DELICOUS! May you be inspired, empowered, and equipped to live a sweet, sassy, and satisfied life...

Surprise!
Guess what? You get one more delicious living tip...

Delicious Living Tip #17
Help other women to become delicious women! Speak and breathe life into the dreams of other women.

Delicious!

100 Tips to Create a Deliciously Vibrant Life

1. Be grateful. Know that you are already prosperous. Showing gratitude for what you already have helps you attract more abundance.

2. Connect with prosperous people and ask yourself, "How can I get more of what they have and then do the work to get it?"

3. Live authentically. If your inner self is in turmoil, it doesn't matter what you portray to the world. You will attract that which reflects your innermost thoughts and feelings.

4. Sit down and write your life's mission statement in ten words or less and begin living by it.

5. Identify the one person or thing in your life that is holding you back, and develop a realistic plan to begin removing it from your life.

6. Create an image of how you want to feel, look, behave and think when you walk into a room full of strangers. What is the silent message you want to send them about you, your spirit, your being?

7. Make it your life goal to create vibrancy in other people's lives. You reap what you sow, and you'll feel good in the process of making other people feel good.

8. Create a sparkle! Does your skin look radiant? Is your smile bright? Is your hair glowing? Do your eyes shine? Put your best face forward. Exfoliate and moisturize your skin, whiten your teeth, get a new haircut or trim. Do whatever makes you happy to create that sparkle that illuminates vibrancy when people meet you.

9. If you had the power to project the vision for your life on a big screen, can you see it clearly? What does it look like?

10. If money were not an issue, what would you be doing and being in life?

11. Identify three things that make you happy, bring you peace, or inspire your creativity. Make a plan to do those things every day or every week.

12. Define what vibrancy means to you. Make it simple, clear, and realistic.

13. Have you ever met someone and said, "Wow, who is that?" or "Wow, I am so glad to be in that person's presence?" Identify what was special about that person, and find specific ways you can create that same or a similar "wow" effect on other people.

14. Think about your current, natural, God-given talents. Bring them forth, polish them, and share them with the world!

15. Music has wonderful and intense healing power. Music inspires us to create, transform, and become energized. Create a CD or tape with inspirational songs… songs that evoke your deepest emotions. Play it when you are feeling down, right before a big event, or whenever you choose.

16. Don't wait for opportunities—create them or kick down the door and make them happen.

17. You are already vibrant, but like the diamond in the rough, you just need a little polishing and refining for your beauty to be revealed and your vibrant shine to come forth. You are worth the work. Invest in your life: instead of buying shoes, buy a book. Instead of buying that mocha latte, save your money and attend a self-development workshop. INVEST in you and elevate to your highest self.

Delicious!

18. Read books on self-discovery and make shifts in your life.

19. Mentor someone. This is a good way to give back and keep the energy and vibration of abundance in steady flow.

20. Do volunteer work in your community. Giving back helps you manifest your desires.

21. Be grateful. Know that you are already prosperous. Showing gratitude for what you already have helps you attract more abundance.

22. Create intention statements for your life and use them every day. This helps your desires to be continuously broadcasted into the universe.

23. Forgive those who have hurt you. Forgiveness allows your spirit to be free and opens the door of receiving.

24. Take care of yourself. When you feel good, look good, and live well, you are able to allow what you desire to come to you.

25. Use that intuitive voice inside to make decisions about your life; it will always lead you in the right direction.

26. Live authentically. If your inner self is in turmoil, it doesn't matter what you portray to the world. You will attract that which reflects your innermost thoughts and feelings.

27. Live like money is not an issue. Allow money to come and go freely. This tells the universe that you trust it will return money to you, thus allowing more money to come your way.

28. Define what your best life looks like. Sit quietly and imagine yourself living your best life. What are you doing, where do you live, who is in your life, how much money do you make, how are you specifically making a contribution to humanity? Envision

yourself doing what you dream of. Where are you? What are people saying? How do you feel? Hold that image and those feelings in your head, really feel the feelings and imagine "it" coming into your being—now let it go! Write down the things you need to do and the people you need to connect with. Set a timeline. Repeat this process several times until you have a simple, clear, and practical plan.

29. If your life was an image or picture, what would it be? This is your logo for your life.

30. If your life were the title of a book, what would it be and why? This is the tagline for your life.

31. If you were a product, what would you be, and what would be your tagline or slogan? This is how you want to be remembered.

32. If you were given 30 seconds to describe what you stand for, what would you say? You need to be able to present or sell yourself in an instant.

33. Remember that your life is your own, and live it by your own standards.

34. When you die, what three things do you want to be remembered for? This is the legacy you want to leave for young women.

35. If you were to compare your life to that of a famous person, who would it be? This is what you should strive to become.

36. When you strip away every title or worldly identifier, who are you really? This should define what lives in your soul.

37. Look around your home or office and see if you have piles and boxes. If so, get the clutter out of your space. The physical signs of clutter are a symbol of the mental clutter you are dealing with.

Delicious!

38. Determine the things you are avoiding in life (people, events, and tasks). Get clear on why you are avoiding them, and take action right now to deal with them.

39. Pay attention to how often you are confused, and try to figure out why you are uncertain. When you are unclear, your blessings are blocked. Open up the channels of receiving.

40. Find at least one person with whom you can honestly and openly discuss the things in your life that are creating mental and emotional clutter. Use them, but don't abuse them.

41. Meditate. Take 15 minutes a day to sit quietly, relax, and breathe deeply.

42. Journal daily. Write whatever comes to mind. Reflect back on your journal daily to see if there are patterns, themes, or solutions to your problems.

43. Resist the urge to procrastinate. When something needs to be done, do it right away. Every moment is an opportunity to create your life.

44. Do self-assessment every day. Ask yourself, "How am I feeling, why am I feeling this way, and what can I do right now to overcome the feelings or obstacles?"

45. Determine what makes you smile and do it often.

46. Spend time with people who make you laugh.

47. Slip into a hot aromatherapy bubble bath at least once a week.

48. Say no to something you don't want to do, and be okay with that. The more you do this, the more authentic you will become.

49. Dig out an old photo album and remember the past. This will help you see who you were, where you are, and what you want out of your future.

Dessert Selections: Tasty Life Tips and Tools

50. Call that old friend that you use to have so much fun with, and reconnect.

51. Eat chocolate and just savor the flavor!

52. Take a drive all by yourself and play your favorite music as loud as you like, or drive in complete silence and just BE with yourself.

53. Go back to your former younger self and spend an hour coloring—yes, in a coloring book with crayons.

54. Discover what makes your heart sing, that thing that makes you tingle inside, and do it often.

55. Just like any other living thing, your soul needs to be nourished. What are you doing to nourish your soul?

56. Spend some quiet time with yourself to reflect on the present moments and be fully awakened in all your senses.

57. Put on your favorite music, sit back in a comfortable chair, and just feel the vibrations of the music.

58. Dust off your favorite book and read it again. This time, intentionally apply what you read in your life.

59. Step outside, on your porch, balcony, or patio and look toward the sky, breathing deeply and just feeling the weather and the moment as it is. You will realize again that there is something bigger and more powerful out there than the problems you may be facing.

60. Go to bed an hour early, and as you lie there waiting to fall asleep, smile with your eyes closed as you reflect on everything you are grateful for.

61. Begin your soul journey by reading *Soul Eruption! An amazing journey of self-discovery.*

62. Use your energy wisely. Don't waste it on procrastinators and those who do not believe in you or your dreams.

Delicious!

63. What would you do for free? Discover it and do it; it's probably your passion and purpose in life.

64. Have you made a list of all the things you want to do before you die? Do it now!

65. When life gives you lemons, sprinkle a little bit of your juicy goodness in the mix and whip up the most fabulous lemon meringue pie you can imagine.

66. Remember that everything that glitters is not gold. Be careful—distractions come in nice, pretty little packages.

67. Do you know your top three core values in life?

68. Do you have a mentor? If you do, are you tapping into their wisdom often? If not, why not?

69. What specifically are you giving back to the world?

70. What makes you feel alive inside?

71. Refuse to show up in the world as anyone but you. Don't waste time trying to be a carbon copy of someone else.

72. Stand in front of the mirror and find five things you truly like about yourself.

73. Call your best friend and ask her to give you an honest assessment of how you are perceived by others. Don't take it personally. Eat the meat and spit out the bones.

74. Focus on strengthening the positive things about yourself.

75. Dig out your resume and polish it up. You never know when a great opportunity will pop up!

76. Browse a thesaurus and discover three new words for the word "good" and begin using them in your daily vocabulary.

77. Ask your boss how you can improve your performance, and gladly do it.

78. Go a whole day without complaining, and see how much more mental energy you have.

79. Get up a half an hour earlier than usual for a week and just sit and reflect on where your life is and where you want it go.

80. Define your own soul scent, and everywhere you go spritz your goodness in the room.

81. Quit worrying about what everyone else will think about you. Just do what you love and be who you want to be.

82. Stop complaining about your life and blaming everyone else for your current lifestyle.

83. You must commit today to discovering your divine purpose and living abundantly. Are you ready to face your fears and take responsibility for your life? Say this out loud: "Today I commit to discovering my purpose and will daily create the reality I desire!"

84. Write down three very specific words to describe how you want to feel about yourself and your life. Choose words that are clear, realistic, and achievable.

85. Go to a mirror right now and look at your reflection. Describe what you see physically and how you feel about yourself on the inside.

86. Do your words match what you feel inside? If so, you have a good start. If not, there is incongruence in your life and you need to seek balance. Congruence is when what's on the inside (feelings/thoughts) matches what's on the outside (actions/behaviors/ physical characteristics). Work to create balance in your mind, body, and spirit.

87. List the toxic things and people in your life. List everything that is keeping you stuck. Circle all the things you have control over, and put an X by the things that you feel you have no control over. First,

Delicious!

focus on the things your circled. Start developing a plan for each one, and do something each day to begin moving that mountain out of your life.

88. Begin to change your thinking. If you think you can't, you won't. If you think it's too late, it is. If you think you don't deserve it, you don't.

89. Take time each day to release the negative energy you absorbed in the day, I call it a "toxic release."

90. Spend time with the people you love. Tell them you love them, but most importantly show them you love them.

91. Take time out each day to reflect upon your life. If you do not like where you stand, think about what you want and take big, bold steps toward it.

92. Discover your greatest physical attribute, then showcase it, play it up, and relish it.

93. Surround yourself with other vibrant women. Can you imagine the glow and energy of this connection? Don't be afraid another vibrant woman will steal your shine, because only you can shine like you do.

94. Discover what is sassy about you and be sassy (alive, assertive, outgoing, and charismatic) at least once or twice a day.

95. Master your craft, whatever it may be. Be the best at what you do, and don't be afraid to showcase your skills.

96. Take your "savvyness" to another dimension. Know your stuff. Be articulate and speak clearly, concisely, and assertively. Be sure people know you deserve to be seen, heard, and valued.

97. Become irresistible. Create an aura that draws people in and leave them begging for more long after you are gone.

Dessert Selections: Tasty Life Tips and Tools

98. Each day brings new opportunities to create your sweet life. Be sure to take action every day to make your dreams a reality.

99. Love yourself. Love your body. Love your curves. Love all the unique features about you. The things that are different are the things you must use to stand out in a crowd.

100. Be delicious! Be so good, look so good, feel so good, speak and walk so good that people will want more of the delicious flavor you bring to the world!

Delicious!

30 Catriceology Actions, Tips, and Strategies to Be Deliciously Magnetic

1. Remember that you are a magnet: you attract what you give energy to and what you think about. Focus on what you want, and surround yourself with people with positive energy.

2. Live in the moment and plan for the future. Being vibrant is a right-now action, and magnetizing only works right now. Magnetize what you want.

3. Look deeply into the eyes of other people. Everything you need to know you will see there. This helps you make a deep, energizing connection with people.

4. If you desire to be attractive (magnetic), you must be transparent and irresistibly authentic.

5. Add a special touch to everything you do with people or for people. This creates an energy of joy and abundance, and people will be attracted to your vibrant energy.

6. Leave a profound effect on others in every engagement. Make people feel good and they will smile inside long after you leave their presence. They will remember the lasting impression you made upon them.

7. Be bold in how you present yourself. Do it with ease, class, and grace. You will create an energetic spark within all those you meet, and they will want to know you and stay connected with you.

8. Learn how to look in the mirror and become mesmerized with yourself. Yes, be in awe of your own wisdom, beauty, and integrity. When you feel attracted to yourself you can easily magnetize others.

9. Live a fulfilling life with no shame. Love your life and spread that love to others by shining brightly so that you may put some sunshine in other people's lives.

10. Give people more than what they ask for. They will be delightfully surprised and you'll emanate energy of love and abundance that come back to you when you need it most and when you least expect it.

11. Create energy of forward movement. Let the energy of creation and destiny pull you forward instead of allowing yourself to be pushed by obligation and fear.

12. Create a daily ritual to rejuvenate your energy source and eliminate the toxins of the day. This is essential to keep your vibrancy healthy and alive.

13. Take care of your emotional, spiritual, and mental needs first. If you want to bring joy and vibrancy to others, you have to make sure your source is plentiful.

14. Leave people with subtle, almost mysterious deposits of vibrancy. Smile with your eyes, give a tender touch, pay close attention to what their unspoken needs are and provide what they need in a subtle way. They will walk away profoundly affected yet wonder "What just happened?" They will seek you out again and again.

15. Do not settle. Ask for what you want and believe you deserve it. Do not put up with the intolerable as this dulls your shine and creates a presence of unattractiveness that slows down your prosperity energy.

16. Show people how to give only vibrancy to you by giving only vibrancy to yourself.

17. Accept your limitations but focus on your strengths. Polish them, showcase them, and let the world know what you stand for and what you are good at. Revel in your personal power.

Delicious!

18. Be fully awakened in every moment. Feel everything, sense everything, and respond to only the things that matter in life. The more you feel what you and others need, the more vibrant and attractive you are.

19. Create a living and working space full of vibrancy. This helps keep your radiant energy flowing and gives you another source of mental, emotional, and spiritual rejuvenation.

20. Pay attention to posture and body language. Stand tall, walk strong, hold your head up, look people in the eyes, speak confidently, smile often, and move through the world as if you are on a mission in life.

21. Be grateful for your past, both the good and the bad; be alive today and excited about tomorrow.

22. Be intentional in every moment. Be unconditionally active in creating the life you desire. Your drive and ambition is attractive and keeps the energy of abundance flowing in your direction.

23. Discover and live by your core values in every moment. Do not stray from them, do not compromise them, because they are the compass for creating a life you love on your own terms.

24. Keep it simple. Don't over-complicate your life with too many small details. Do what makes you feel alive inside, and stay focused on the things that matter to you most.

25. Discover what you are good at and master it. Polish your craft, make improvements, and keep evolving into the most phenomenal woman you can become.

26. Always speak in your authentic voice. Tell the truth and speak and act with integrity. Integrity is doing what you *say* you will do, even when no one is watching.

27. Make sure the vision for your life is crystal-clear. It must be so vividly clear that when you speak about it people do not have to question what it is that you mean or are talking about. Visionaries naturally lead others towards their greatness. When you can inspire others to follow you, you know you are a vibrant, magnetic person.

28. See people for who they really are. Do not be fooled by what anyone tells you, but be led by how they behave. Align with those who behave with vibrancy.

29. Be genuine in all your interactions and expressions. When people see you for who you really are, they will more likely be attracted to you.

30. Love hard. Love deeply. Laugh often, sometimes at yourself. Dream big and chase your dreams and tackle them to the ground. Celebrate daily. Celebrate every small yet fabulous thing about yourself. Live your life like it's *deliciously* golden!

Delicious!

The Seven Laws of Delicious Living Success

Delicious Law #1: *Stop letting other people, events, and life situations control who you are or who you want to become.*
You absolutely do not need anyone's permission to live your life. You are the one who walks in that skin, so quit worrying about what everyone thinks or what they might say about the decisions you make in life. Refuse to give up your power to choose how you will live your life, who will come along for the journey, and where you will end up. It's your life! If you don't make it delicious, who will?

"The question isn't who is going to let me; it's who is going to stop me." —*Ayn Rand*

Delicious Law #2: *Quit living in fear, doubt, and worry!* That's right: agonizing over things you cannot control is simply a waste of your time. Failure to face your fears only makes them bigger and stronger, so stare fear in the face and say "Bring it on." Some say when life gives you lemons, make lemonade. I say when life gives you lemons make a fabulous lemon meringue pie, with lots of whipped cream and a sweet cherry on top!

"Do the one thing you think you cannot do. Fail at it. Try again. Do better the second time. The only people who never tumble are those who never mount the high wire. This is your moment. Own it."
—*Oprah Winfrey*

Delicious Law #3: *Dream BIG and have even bigger faith.* You must realize that the only limits on your life are the ones you impose upon yourself. Who says you are not destined for greatness? Who says you can't make six figures or drive a BMW? Who says you can't travel the world? The only person who blocks your delicious destiny is you, so tell yourself to get out of the way and boldly step into your sassy stilettos and walk it out!

"I love to see a young girl go out and grab the world by the lapels. Life's a bitch. You've got to go out and kick ass." —Maya Angelou

Delicious Law #4: Take control of your thoughts. Think your way to the life you desire. Thoughts control your feelings, feelings control your actions, and your actions create your destiny. Get rid of those old mental tapes that speak fear and stagnation in your life and replace them with delicious thoughts of the sweetest life you can imagine. Focus your mental energy on you, your dreams, and your life. You can do that with three actions:

Action #1: Learn the art of "being" versus doing. Focus your thoughts, actions, and behaviors on being in the moment and relishing the splendor of life. When you spend your life "doing," you miss the simple wonders of happiness.

Action #2: Stop looking for the big moment or breakthrough in your life. Instead, create the life you want right now in this moment. A breakthrough is not coming; it is in the present moment.

Action #3: Focus on BEING authentically YOU. Be intentional about everything you do! Become consumed with becoming your BEST SELF and doing what you LOVE. When you do this, you have little time to worry about what others think or what they are doing.

The power of thought is one of the greatest gifts you'll ever receive. Use your thoughts to create a life so tantalizing that other people will want a piece of it.

"Your thoughts and beliefs of the past have created this moment, and all the moments up to this moment. What you are now choosing to believe and think and say will create the next moment and the next day and the next month and the next year." —Louise Hay

Delicious!

Delicious Law #5: ***Discover your "it," master it, and shamelessly flaunt it to the world.*** Living a delicious life is about discovering the vibrant YOU within and not being afraid to simply just be you all the time and in any situation. You were given a beautiful light, a light to shine so that others may be lifted up in the darkness. You have special gifts uniquely designed for your life, and it is your duty to use those gifts to heal and inspire the world. So go ahead, discover your "it" and tantalize the world with it.

"We ask ourselves, who am I to be brilliant, gorgeous, talented, and fabulous? Actually, who are you not to be? You are a child of God. Your playing small doesn't serve the world. There's nothing enlightened about shrinking so that other people won't feel insecure around you. We are all meant to shine, as children do. We are born to make manifest the glory of God that is within us. It's not just in some of us, it's in everyone. And as we let our own light shine, we unconsciously give other people permission to do the same. As we are liberated from our own fear, our presence automatically liberates others." —Marianne Williamson

153

Delicious Law #6: ***Reinvent yourself each day.*** Just like a piece of succulent fruit, sometimes you've got to peel away a thick outer shell to get to the juicy goodness. You are filled with juicy goodness, and it's time for you to release your bursting flavor into the world. Evolution is a process that can sometimes be painful. Just like the caterpillar bound in the cocoon, you too may have dark moments in your life, but if you do the work from the inside out, I guarantee that you will transform into a beautiful butterfly. It's your choice: stay a caterpillar and be bound in darkness forever, or get yourself right from the inside out and break free as a beautiful butterfly and fly forever!

Start today by creating a ritual for your life instead of following a routine. A ritual is celebratory, and a routine is obligatory. A ritual includes sacred and special time for you to reflect, reposition, rejuvenate, and restore your spirit. A ritual brings joy and satisfaction. Add one thing new to your ritual every week to create a life ritual that helps you become your highest, best, and most delicious self.

"Although beauty may be in the eye of the beholder, the feeling of being beautiful exists solely in the mind of the beheld."
—*Martha Beck*

Delicious Law #7: Stop making excuses and just live your life!

Excuses lead to immobilization, dissatisfaction, and failure. Learn to embrace "I am willing" as the key to unlocking the possibilities, opportunities, and doorways to a sweet, satisfying, and scrumptious life. If you knew behind Door Number 1 there was a million dollars and a key was offered to you, would you open the door NOW or later? A delicious and fulfilling life is more valuable than a million dollars. Don't search for the keys; you already have them. If you cannot say you are living a delicious life it's as simple as saying, "I am willing to do what it takes, to stop making excuses, and to stop procrastinating in my life." Then you must take action. Open up your life pantry, browse around and pull out your best ingredients and create the most delicious life you could ever imagine.

"When life presents challenges, stand up, stare them in the face and say 'I am victorious, you do not have control of my life' and then charge at them will full force (mind, body, and spirit). The goal of a delicious life is to live without limits, restrictions, or fear!"

Delicious!

Create Your "Sweet Life" List

Use this page and the next to create a list of all the things you want to do in your lifetime:

1.

2.

3.

4.

5.

6.

Dessert Selections: Tasty Life Tips and Tools

7.

8.

9.

10.

This is just the beginning. Take some time to sit quietly and reflect on your life. I encourage you to create a list of at least 100 delectable things you want to do or accomplish in your lifetime. Dream deliciously big!

Delicious!

25 Questions to Help You Begin Creating Your Delicious Life

Take some time to reflect upon each of the questions below and jot down a few notes, comments, ideas, and thoughts. For the "yes" or "no" questions, don't just write down one-word answers. For each "no," write down reasons why you're not doing what the question asks, along with some thoughts about what you would need to do to change the "no" to a "yes." If the answer is "yes," write down how you could do it or live it more vibrantly.

1. Am I living the life of my dreams?

2. Is my life in balance?

3. Is someone or something controlling my life other than me?

4. What are my biggest fears?

5. Am I willing to take a deep look into my soul and discover why I exist?

Delicious!

6. How am I showing gratitude in my life?

7. Am I giving back to the world?

8. If I could do anything and have my provisions met, what would I be doing?

9. Who is creating stress in my life?

10. Do I wake up excited about the day or dread getting out of bed?

11. What makes me feel alive inside?

12. Am I living in faith or living in fear?

Delicious!

13. If I lose my job, do I have a backup plan?

14. Have I created my sweet life list (a list of the things I want to do, experience, and accomplish in life before I die)? (See pages 155–156.)

15. Am I living in the moment or stuck in the past?

16. Is my life pulsating with energy?

17. If I don't wake up tomorrow morning, have I done everything I wanted to?

18. What is the vision for my life?

Delicious!

19. Have I identified the people who are in my life for a reason, a season, and a lifetime?

20. Am I ready to take back my life?

21. Do I speak my truth every day?

22. Is my spirit authentic?

23. Am I listening to my authentic voice?

24. Who am I allowing to steal my emotional energy?

25. Am I working a job or loving my career?

Delicious!

10 Right-Now Actions to Become More Delicious

1. Turn up your social and intuitive radar. Pay close attention to what you are feeling rather than what you are thinking. Listen with your eyes—people will tell you everything you need to know with their body language.

2. Begin listening to your intuitive voice and respond to it. Most likely it will lead you in the right direction.

3. What one thing can you do right now to change the direction of your life, to begin living a life you love? Do it now, even if you are afraid.

4. If you haven't been keeping a journal, start today. If you are seeking to create a life you love, live with more passion and purpose, journaling will help reveal what really matters in life and the patterns that may be keeping you stuck in place.

5. What one area of your life is most intact? How can you use your strengths in this area to create balance and harmony in the other areas of your life?

6. Put your best face forward! Do you have a regular skin care ritual? If not, it's time to reveal your vibrant glow! There are four essential steps to radiant skin: cleanse, tone, repair, and moisturize. Discover Sensaria® for a new way to love the skin you're in.

Dessert Selections: Tasty Life Tips and Tools

7. Go to bed with soothing sounds and wake up feeling refreshed! Put your CD player by the bed, pop in a relaxing CD to fall asleep with more ease, and wake up ready for the world.

8. Create a spa day at home. Get rid of the kids and the significant other and unwind. Light candles and slip into an aromatherapy bath. Sit back and reflect on how you WILL begin living your life with no limits!

9. Sit down and answer the following question: "Where do I want to be in life, and how do I want to be in life this time next year?" Make your answer clear and intentional, and start your new path right now.

10. Identify the ONE person who inspires you the most and connect with that person today. Ask for tips on how you can do what they do, have what they have, and BE how they are.

Delicious!

About the Author

Catrice Jackson, speaker, life designer and master chef extraordinaire, is simply a woman who has "for sure" discovered her passion and purpose for living. Catrice has been an avid and active advocate of women's empowerment for over 20 years and has dedicated her life to sharing her gift of inspiration and empowerment to women across the globe. Catrice's personal mission is to speak and breathe delicious life into every woman she encounters. Catrice believes that every woman deserves to live the life of her dreams, and she is on an international mission to help every woman create and live a delicious life. Catrice has accepted her divine calling and is taking the world by storm with her sassy, unique, and fresh way of living, *Catriceology: Becoming delicious from the inside out*. Catrice Jackson lives her life out loud and is dedicated to helping YOU define, create, and live your most delicious life ever.

Get Catriceology and Live the Delicious Life...

- For updates on Catriceology, The Lifestyle of the Delicious Woman, sign up to receive the Delicious Woman newsletter at www.catriceologyenterprises.com
- Want a personalized delicious life design? You bring the ingredients and I'll bring the recipe. Together we'll create a scrumptious life. For life design sessions, contact Catrice at www.catriceologyenterprises.com
- To book Catrice for your next event, submit your speaking request at www.catricemjackson.com
- Stay tuned to Catriceology Enterprises for upcoming events, special offers, and the new Catriceology Culinary School for fabulous telecourses and webinars.

Catrice M. Jackson, M.S., LMHP, LPC

Catriceology Enterprises

Author, Speaker, Life Designer, and Master Chef
Extraordinaire

"The Speaker and Life Designer You Choose When You
Are READY to Live and Work Deliciously"

One Platform...One Stage... One Mike....
One Message...Millions Transformed

Choose Catrice M. Jackson for your next event and make
it *delicious!*

Guaranteed to show up and show out

Living Vibrantly Delicious Blog:
http://catriceslivingdeliciously.blogspot.com/

Catriceology Enterprises:
www.catriceologyenterprises.com

Catrice Jackson Speaks:
www.catricejacksonspeaks.com

Catrice's Delicious Life Institute:
www.catricemjackson.com

Delicious!